How NOT to Lose Your Home
When Life Happens…

How NOT to Lose Your Home
When Life Happens…

LaTonya S. Johnson

Solutions by TJ
BehindOnMortgagePayments.com
2019

Copyright © 2019 by LaTonya S. Johnson

All rights reserved. This book or any portion thereof may not be reproduced or used in any manner whatsoever without the express written permission of the publisher except for the use of brief quotations in a book review or scholarly journal.

First Printing: 2008

ISBN 978-0-578-22075-8

NSF Holdings, LLC
d/b/a Solutions by TJ
16770 Imperial Valley Rd.
Houston, TX 77060
www.BehindOnMortgagePayments.com

Disclaimer

The data contained in this manual is deemed reliable but not guaranteed. Every effort has been made to ensure the accuracy of this data., BehindOnMortgagePayments.com makes NO WARRANTY or guarantee, expressed or implied, concerning the accuracy or reliability of the content of this manual or of other resources mentioned herein. This information should be used for informational purposes only and does not constitute legal advice. The information provided within this manual is broad in nature, and legal problems are often complex. If you have a legal question, please contact an attorney in your state. Assessing accuracy and reliability of information is the responsibility of the user. BehindOnMortgagePayments.com disclaims any responsibility or liability for any direct or indirect damages resulting from the use of this data. We hope this information provides you with a valuable tool in saving your home from foreclosure.

Ordering Information:

Special discounts are available on quantity purchases by corporations, associations, educators, and others. For details, contact the publisher at the above listed address.

U.S. trade bookstores and wholesalers: Please contact BehindOnMortgagePayments.com
Tel: (713) 903-7107 or email support@BehindOnMortgagePayments.com

Dedication

To my beautiful daughter and all the homeowners who I've helped along the way. Thank you for being my constant motivation to educate, lead and serve.

CONTENTS

ACKNOWLEDGEMENTS XIII

PREFACE XV

INTRODUCTION 1

    THE BANK DOES NOT WANT YOUR HOUSE 1

WHAT IS FORECLOSURE? 5

STOPPING FORECLOSURE: WHAT'S YOUR 20? 9

    THE PLAYERS 10

    THE DOCUMENTS 10

    THE PROCESS 11

    THE STRATEGY 14

        HAVE YOU RECEIVED THE FIRST LETTER? 14

        HAVE YOU RECEIVED THE SECOND LETTER? 14

LENDER ACTIONS THAT COULD STOP OR DELAY FORECLOSURE 17

OPTIONS TO SAVE YOUR HOME 19

    OTHER SOURCES OF FUNDING 19

        CREDIT UNION 19

        PERSONAL PROPERTY LOANS 20

        FIND A ROOMMATE/ AIRBNB 20

        BECOME AN ENTREPRENEUR 20

LIQUIDATE ASSETS 20

RECLAIM DEPOSITS 21

INCOME TAX REFUND 21

INSURANCE 21

CREDIT CARDS 22

PAYPAL 22

GOOGLE 22

RETIREMENT FUND 22

REFINANCE WITH A CO-MORTGAGOR 23

BILL DEFERRMENT 24

FRIENDS AND RELATIVES 24

CONTEST PROPERTY TAXES 24

SOCIAL ORGANIZATIONS 26

DEBT CONSOLIDATION 26

DEBT CONSOLIDATION LOANS 26

LENDER RELATED FORECLOSURE OPTIONS 29

FORBEARANCE 29

TEMPORARY INDULGENCE 30

SOLDIERS' AND SAILORS' RELIEF ACT OF 1940 30

REPAYMENT PLAN 31

LOAN MODIFICATION 31

LOAN RESTRUCTURING 32

PARTIAL CLAIM 33

REFINANCING 33

DEED IN-LIEU OF FORECLOSURE 34

NATURAL DISASTER 34

HOW TO KNOW WHEN IT IS TIME TO SELL YOUR HOUSE 37

TAKE THE FOLLOWING ACTIONS IMMEDIATELY! 38

HOW TO SHORT SELL YOUR HOUSE FOR MAXIMUM PROFIT 38

LOCATING BUYERS 39

LOCATING A REALTOR 39

LOCATING AN INVESTOR 40

YOUR HOME'S MARKET VALUE 41

HOW TO DEVELOP A BOTTOM-LINE SELLING POSITION 42

MARKET ANALYSIS 42

CLOSING COSTS 46

FOR SALE SUMMARY 50

SELLER FINANCING OPTIONS 51

LOAN ASSUMPTION 51

CONTRACT FOR DEED 51

BANKRUPTCY 53

CHAPTER 7-LIQUIDATION 53

CHAPTER 11-REORGANIZATION 54

CHAPTER 13- ADJUSTMENT OF DEBTS OF AN INDIVIDUAL WITH REGULAR INCOME 55

FORECLOSURE AUCTION 57

THE PLAYERS 57

THE DOCUMENTS 57

THE PROCESS 58

STRATEGY 58

HOW TO PREPARE 59

CHALLENGE THE LOAN DOCUMENTS 60

REAL ESTATE SETTLEMENT PROCEDURES ACT (RESPA) 60

REGULATION Z 62

CONVERSATION LOG 69

REFERRALS 69

CONVERSATION: 69

APPENDIX 72

FORECLOSURE ASSISTANCE 72

WORKBOOK 72

ONLINE FORECLOSURE WEBINARS FOR HOMEOWNERS 72

SHORT SALE CONSULTATION 72

INVESTOR PROGRAM 73

PRODUCT & SERVICES PRICING 73

IMPORTANT INFORMATION ABOUT HOUSING COUNSELING 74

INTERNET RESOURCES 75

SOCIAL ORGANIZATIONS: MONETARY ASSISTANCE 76

REFERENCES 81

ACKNOWLEDGEMENTS

I would like to thank my daughter, Madison Hall, for giving me the motivation to keep pushing forward and striving to be the best person that I can be. I would also like to thank Robert Glaspie (best friend, life coach and my own personal Superman) and Neal Brooks (graphic designer, consultant and foreclosure client). Without their help this book would never have been completed.

Thank you for your patience and guidance, and use of your brilliant minds...

PREFACE

The Best Time to Prepare Is Before A Serious Situation Occurs

Am I right about it?

That's why we purchase insurance policies for our health, home, auto, etc.; to cover our backs IN CASE an incident happens.

I'm certain that if you own a home, then you have homeowner's insurance. Why, because lenders require that you maintain a policy.

But what will you do when an event occurs that is not covered by conventional insurance? An event like a major illness or disability, job loss, divorce or a natural disaster outside the covered flood zones…

I pray that none of those things happen to you.

But IF THEY DO…

Do you have a plan?

Do you know what to do if you can no longer pay your mortgage in accordance with the agreements that you signed at closing?

I'll be the first to raise my hand and let you know that I had NO CLUE of what to do…

In 2007 I was a serial entrepreneur. I owned a restaurant, an office building for attorneys and invested in real estate. I was also pregnant with my now 12-year-old daughter, Madison (the picture above is just one of my favorites).

All was well until I started having complications in my pregnancy and the market crashed. Lenders stopped giving out loans and the entire real estate market came to (what seemed like) an abrupt halt.

I had a severe case of the "Mommy Brain." Looking back, I believe that it was God's way of saving my baby, because I could no longer think and execute a plan or even formulate thoughts of worry. All that I was able to think about was… breathe in… breathe out. I was no longer able to work in the restaurant or on real estate; which were my two streams of income at the time.

So gradually the money stopped flowing in, all of my savings were used and at 6 months pregnant… I could not even afford a pair of maternity underwear.

I felt completely overwhelmed every time I tried to Force my brain to think. My heart would begin to pound out of my chest and my baby would start moving around frantically. Then it literally felt like God would up the "Mommy Brain" chemicals even more. By the time I had Madison, I couldn't even figure out how to put on my shoes…

My home went into foreclosure, I filed bankruptcy, lost my cars, lost my businesses and my man.

I did not have a plan. I did not want to talk to my lender or other creditors because I didn't have the money to pay them so why keep saying the same darn thing. The most important thing that I did not know… were my options.

And that is what propelled me to create this workbook. I want you to have a Plan B. I want you to have information readily available regarding options to save your home for foreclosure…when life happens.

INTRODUCTION

My job is to help you identify the option that works best for you and teach you how to keep as much of your equity as possible. Your job is to simply remain open-minded.
I lost my home to foreclosure in 2008, so I understand what you're going through. None of us are born with step-by-step guidebooks on how to handle life's challenges, that's why I created BehindonMortgagePayments.com and this workbook. Both of which are swift, to the point and easy to understand. I simply want to offer information that will help you to Think Clearly, understand your options and make informed decisions on how to move forward. I don't want another person to ever feel as lost and helpless as I did.

THE BANK DOES NOT WANT YOUR HOUSE

As you read through this manual, keep in mind that lenders would rather work with you to find *any* reasonable solution than to foreclose. Their risk and costs are far too great. See, lenders are in the business of lending money - not obtaining real estate. They make money by collecting funds lent to borrowers plus interest. Therefore, the lender would rather work out a plan, than to foreclose and lose profit. Regardless of the value of your home or the amount of equity accumulated, banks lose money when they must take a property from the owner in order to satisfy a debt. Here is an example of the amount of money that lenders may lose when they must foreclose on a mortgage for $125,000 with a six percent (6%) interest rate:

Expenses:

Pre-Foreclosure Sale

- Inspection Fees $45.00
- BPO Fee $200.00
- Attorney Fees $1,000.00
- Foreclosure Costs $500.00
- Property Preservation $200.00

Post Foreclosure Sale

- Repair Costs $2,500.00
- Marketing Costs $7,500.00

Lost Income

- Loan Interest (6mo @ 6%) $4,800.00
- Late Fees ($35/mo) $210.00

Total $16,955.00

When you take into account that the lender may be forced to sell at a discount of up to 30% of the assessed value (which is based on a BPO or Brokers Price Opinion) obtained as a result of the default, their losses could range from $17,000 to $38,000 based on this scenario. Research commissioned by the Joint Economic Committee of Congress revealed an average foreclosure costs of $58,759 per loan, in comparison to the cost of foreclosure prevention which averaged $3,300.

So even though the situation may look bleak, and it appears as though you are so deep in the hole that you'll never recover, remember that just about *any* reasonable plan will be accepted. Keep reading because you may find an unexpected answer. If you cannot afford to keep the house, read on. Suggestions will be provided to help you to identify other options.

However, if you don't want to read another word, please take heed to the following advice:

Don't lose hope. Unless your house has been sold at auction, you still have options.

Lastly, take action immediately! The foreclosure clock is ticking if a notice of default has been filed. If you choose to do nothing, you will lose your home, severely damage your credit rating, there may be tax consequences, and you will possibly still owe the lender if the house is sold at auction for less than you owe. Do not wait until the last minute. **Your options decrease as time progresses**, so seek help today.

> GO Make every effort to save your home and credit history if at all possible.

> GO Contact your mortgage lender immediately to identify what options are available to save your property. (See Pages 29-35)

> STOP Do not vacate the property. If you do, you may be disqualified for certain forms of assistance.

> GO Seek professional advice from an attorney, CPA, credit counselor, or real estate professional that specializes in foreclosures or real estate prior to making a final decision. If you cannot afford to pay someone immediately, there are several groups that provide volunteer services or payment plans. Contact BehindOnMortgagePayments.com or a HUD-approved housing counselor and review the Appendix to obtain a list of local contacts.

We know that you've received lots of mail, and even people knocking on your door stating that they would like to "help" you. Some of these individuals do approach you with a sincere heart to help. However, be careful because there are others who will prey on your lack of knowledge and steal your home… with your consent if you don't understand the things that I'm teaching you. That's why this workbook is so important. We teach you what others don't want you to know.

 Here's some good advice…. If you choose to permanently relieve yourself of the mortgage, sell the house out right. DO NOT DEED THE PROPERTY TO SOMEONE ELSE BEFORE SEEKING LEGAL COUNSEL AND DRAFTING A CONTRACT THAT PROTECTS YOU FROM LOSSES.

God bless you, and you will be in my prayers.

Now let's get on the road to saving your home...

WHAT IS FORECLOSURE?

Prior to executing your options, you must have some idea of what's going on and where you are in the process.

So exactly what is foreclosure?

Foreclosure is the legal process used by lenders to force the sale of your home to repay your mortgage obligation. The process can begin as soon as one mortgage payment is delinquent, however a notice is usually filed after five (5) or six (6) missed payments.

The first action that we suggest for all homeowners that are currently in or are approaching foreclosure, is to take an honest look at your finances and ask the following questions:

1) If you are currently working, how much income do I bring in monthly?
2) Do I foresee a raise, bonus, or any long-term increase in income in the near future?
3) Do I have any outstanding liens (mechanics liens, tax liens, 2nd/3rd mortgage liens, etc.) against the house?
4) Where can I find short-term sources of cash?
5) How much do I pay per month on bills?
6) How can I reduce my monthly bills?
7) Do I honestly have enough money at the end of the month to pay my current mortgage or to increase my monthly payments?
8) Can I really afford to keep the house?

You can afford to keep the house if you have (or will soon have) the income to support mortgage payments. If not, refer to page 37 for additional details and guidance.

The flowchart that follows will help you to identify where you are, and what your options are at each step. As you read through this manual, periodically come back to this chart to see how it fits into your final game plan.

If you are not currently working, ask yourself the following questions:

1) When do I foresee getting a job?
2) If I haven't gotten a job by then, what is my plan B?
3) On what date will I implement Plan B if I'm still not working?

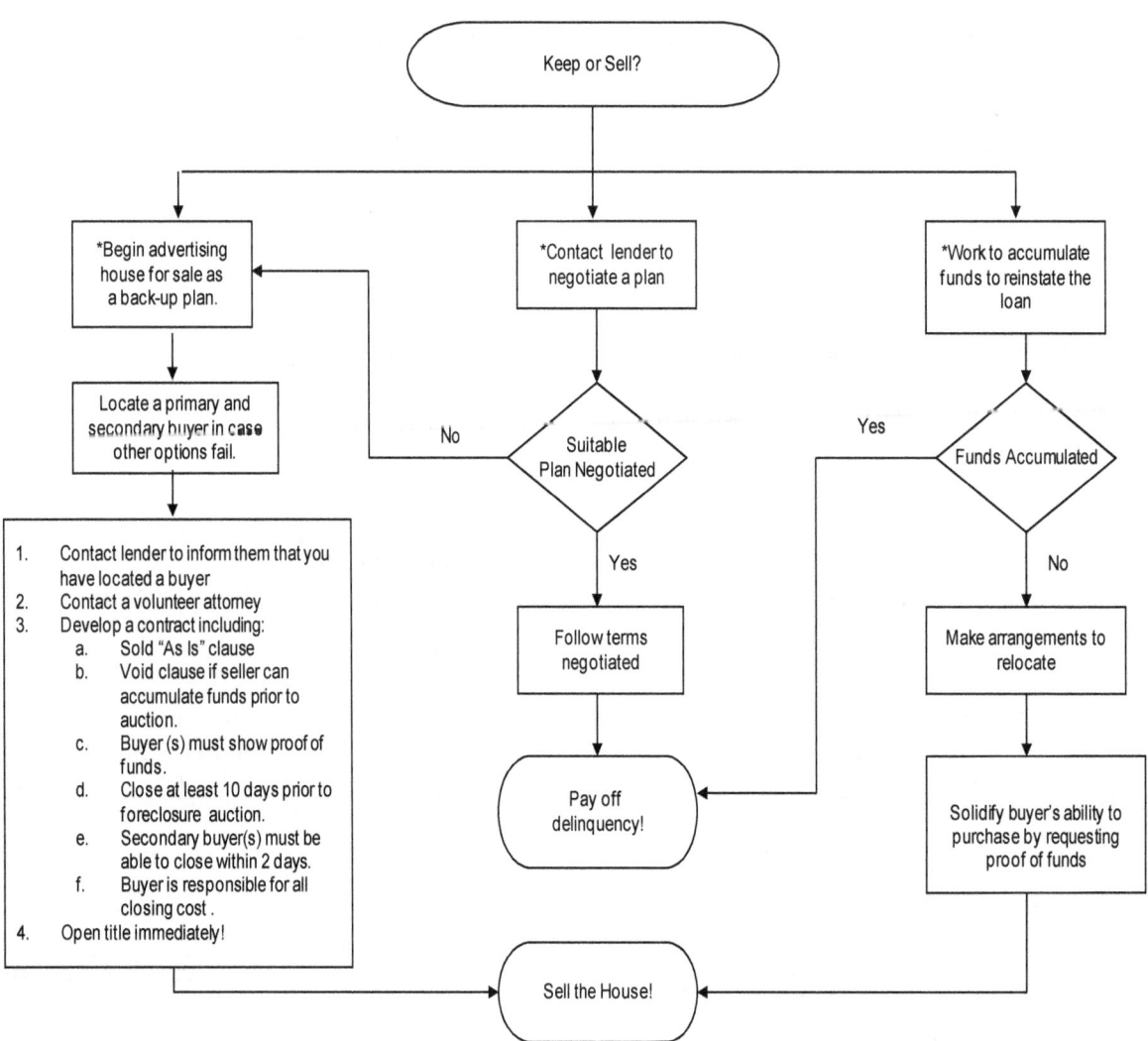

This flow chart suggests that you do three things simultaneously:

1) Contact your lender to see what plans they have available. Later in this workbook (on pages 29-35) we'll discuss the most common options so that you are prepared prior to calling.

2) Work to accumulate the funds to begin making regular payments based on whatever you work out with your lender.

   NOTE: There are options to lower your monthly payment and place all missed payments at the back end of the loan. So, I'm definitely not saying that you must come up with the full amount. However, the lender cannot approve a workout plan until you show that you'll be able to honor the new payment amount.

3) Advertise your house for sale. In some states, including Texas, the foreclosure process only lasts about forty-one (41) days after it begins. That means you can lose your

house in a little over a month…so you have to implement multiple strategies at the same time; **just in case** the others don't work out. The earlier you begin to advertise- the more equity you can negotiate to keep. Plus, you preserve your credit, so that you can buy another house when your circumstances change.

NOTE: Advertising your house for sale does not mean that you have to sell it. You're simply keeping your options open in case there are no other options available.

To fully assess where you are, you must understand your monthly income and expenses. This is one of the items that the lender will request, so go on and get it over with. You can complete the cash flow table and calculation that follows or visit BehindOnMortgagePayments.com/lender-docs to access and excel spreadsheet that does all the calculations for you.

MONTHLY CASH FLOW TABLE

CURRENT INCOME

Source	Amount ($)

CURRENT EXPENSES

Source	Amount ($)

Total Income		Total Expenses	

Total Income - Total Expenses = Positive/Negative Cash Flow

_____ - _____ = _____ (Your Cash Flow)

🛑 If a negative number is generated from this calculation, then identify a method of increasing your income or decreasing expenses. Otherwise, you will not be able to sustain your current lifestyle, and foreclosure or bankruptcy will be an imminent outcome. The good thing about this exercise is that it helps you to see just how much house you can afford, and what payment works best for you. As you continue reading, suggestions will be given to help you to brainstorm how to increase your income, find quick sources of cash, and decrease your expenses.

If you cannot afford to keep your house, cut back for a while. For your own mental health, it is very important that you don't look at cutting back as the end of the world; it is a temporary situation.

Just think about it...isn't it far more advantageous to downgrade from a large house to a smaller one or from a house to an apartment, than to face financial ruin and be forced to live under a bridge? That may be a bit extreme, but the point is for you to keep telling yourself that this situation is temporary. And it will be temporary as long as you work diligently towards rebuilding your finances. You are a courageous and awesome person, and you are capable of shaking the dust off and Pressing On!

--Calvin Coolidge said it best:

"Nothing in the world can take the place of persistence. Talent will not; nothing is more common than unsuccessful men with talent. Genius will not; unrewarded genius is almost a proverb. Education will not. The world is full of educated derelicts. Persistence and determination alone are omnipotent. The slogan, 'Press on,' has solved and always will solve the problems of the human race."

STOPPING FORECLOSURE

Let's use the analogy of taking a road trip to simplify this information.

The first step to stopping foreclosure is to look at your documents (the map) and figure out where you are in the process. You must know who the players are, understand the rules of the road and be aware of where you are at all times throughout the journey. Where you are is Your 20.

This includes where you are as it relates to your personal finances as well as where you are in the foreclosure process. Until you understand these fundamentals, it's nearly impossible to get to your final destination.

Which is out of foreclosure and either keeping your home or selling it for maximum cash in your pocket.

Most people don't consider foreclosure a journey, but it actually is. Here's how…

In every journey, there is a:

- driver
- vehicle
- road map or GPS
- starting point,
- signs along the way,
- pit stops
- other drivers
- law enforcement officers and a
- destination.

As it relates to our discussion:

- You are the driver.
- Your house is the vehicle.
- I am your GPS and this workbook serves as a road map
- Your starting point (Your 20) is likely that you're experiencing financial difficulties or lender errors have occurred and you are currently in or are headed toward foreclosure.
- Signs along the way include documents and phone calls from your lender.
- The law enforcement officer is your lender (though they generally do all that they can to help you to keep your house---but work with me here)
- And the destination is out of or avoiding foreclosure.

Your chances of reaching your destination will greatly increase if you understand the foreclosure process and know your options.

Now do you see how foreclosure is like a journey? People commonly say that they are going through foreclosure. Because one way or another, you will come out of this. My job is to give you directions, so that you can navigate through this process and come out with the best possible scenario.

To begin, let's discuss the process. The easiest way to do this is to start with a few definitions and then go directly into the mechanics of the game.

THE PLAYERS

Mortgagor/Trustor: The borrower in a mortgage agreement who pledges property as security for debt.

Mortgagee/Beneficiary: The lender or creditor in a mortgage agreement.

Trustee: One who holds legal title (i.e. the deed) to property for the benefit of another, or to oversee performance of an obligation by making sure that timely payments are made (title company, escrow company, or the trust company).

Investor: One who commits capital (cash) in order to obtain an increase in cash value over a given time period.

THE DOCUMENTS

Title: Written evidence of the right to or ownership in property. Relating to real estate, the title deed indicates the history of ownership and transfers. It also specifies the name of the individual(s) who have absolute rights to the property. Title may be acquired through purchase, inheritance, devise, gift, or through foreclosure of a mortgage.

Deed: The document by which title to real property is transferred or conveyed from one party to another.

Deed of Trust: A type of security instrument in which the borrower conveys title of real property to a third party (trustee) to be held in trust as security of repayment for the lender, with the provision that the trustee shall reconvey the title to the borrower upon full payment of the debt, and, conversely, will sell the property and pay the debt (foreclose) in the event of a default by the borrower.

Mortgage: The document used as evidence of a pledge of property, usually real property, as security for a debt. In many states, including Texas, this document is a deed of trust. The document may contain the terms of repayment of the debt. The term "mortgage" may be used to describe both the mortgage document itself as well as the separate promissory note showing the loan amount and the terms of repayment.

Promissory Note: A document signed by a borrower promising to repay a loan under agreed-upon terms and procedures.

Power of Sale: A provision in a deed of trust or mortgage that empowers a trustee, without court order, to sell property in the event of default by the mortgagor and to apply the proceeds of the sale to satisfy the obligation, the costs of invoking the procedure, and the expenses of the sale.

DRIVING CITATIONS

Notice of Default: A letter forwarded by the lender notifying the borrower that he/she has 20 days to pay all back payments or the note will be accelerated.

Notice of Acceleration: A letter forwarded by the Trustee notifying the borrower that the loan has been accelerated (i.e. the full balance is due) and will be sold in 21 days. The notice should tell where the notice is recorded as well as the volume and page. It should also state the name of the mortgagor, mortgagee and trustee; as well as the date, time, terms and place of the sale.

Trustee's Deed: When the property is sold at auction, the new owner receives this document as conveyance of ownership.

THE PROCESS

To assist you with this concept we'll take a look at Linda's situation. Review the following synopsis as an illustration of the process:

Linda decides to purchase a house in the state of Texas. So she goes to ABC Bank in order to obtain a loan. She qualifies for the loan and goes to closing in order to finalize the deal. At closing, two documents are presented to Linda for her to sign. The first document is the Deed of Trust (Depending on the state that you are in, a Deed of Trust or a Mortgage will be used. Texas uses a Deed of Trust). Linda signs the Deed of Trust as a means of assuring repayment. By signing this document, she ultimately says that she agrees to convey title to a third party (the trustee) until she has paid for the loan in full. However, if she stops making mortgage payments, the trustee can take the house in order to repay the loan. She also signs a Promissory Note which is merely a promise to repay the loan according to the agreed upon terms (the time during which Linda makes monthly payments) and conditions (interest rate, payment amount, etc.) The bank then receives a signed copy of the promissory note and the trustee receives the Deed of Trust.

Four years after buying the house, Linda gets laid off from her job. Over a six-month period, her savings begin to grow thin, so she skips four (4) mortgage payments. The lender then notifies the trustee that Linda is in default. The trustee then starts the foreclosure process and ultimately sells the house (under the powers granted to him or her in the Deed of Trust) pending her continued failure to repay the debt.

This is the foreclosure process that Linda went through in the state of Texas, without ever going to court:

Forty-one (41) days prior to the foreclosure auction, Linda receives a Demand Letter (also called a Notice of Default or a Notice of Breach) from the Trustee via certified mail. The letter is mailed to her last known address (as shown in the lender's records), so luckily, she has not vacated the property. At this point, she has 20 days to catch up on all missed payments before the bank proceeds with foreclosure.

The 20-day time period passes, and Linda was not able to accumulate the funds. She is now approaching the fifth (5th) missed payment when she receives a 21-day foreclosure notice (also called a Notice of Acceleration). The Acceleration Notice is the lender's way of informing Linda that the entire balance of the loan is due within 21 days of the letter's postmark. This letter provides information regarding the date, place and earliest time that the house will be sold at the foreclosure auction.

The Trustee simultaneously files the foreclosure notice with the county clerk and posts a public record that Linda's house is now in foreclosure at the county courthouse also twenty-one (21) days before the foreclosure auction.

After twenty-one (21) days, Linda was still unable to come up with the funds. Therefore, her house was sold to the highest all cash bidder at an auction on the courthouse steps (which must take place on the first Tuesday of any month (usually between 10:00 am and 4:00 pm), regardless of holidays such as the Fourth of July, Christmas or New Year's.

Following the sale, title is transferred to the new owner (more than likely an investor) by means of a Trustee's Deed.

If the house is sold at auction for less than the amount of Linda's delinquent balance, she is responsible for repaying the difference between fair market value and the balance owed on the loan. Fair market value is the price at which a particular house will sell for in its current condition within 30 to 60 days.

Linda's best plan of action at this point is to acquire evidence verifying the market value of her home. This will ensure that the deficiency is kept at a minimum. If it is not, she should PROTEST by showing proof of the actual market value. The best way to obtain information about the market value is to contact an appraiser if you have at least $300-$375 a local realtor. There are several realtors listed in the Yellow Pages.

Remember, Learn the Clock, Know the Game and Act Timely!

Linda could have saved her home from being sold anywhere in the foreclosure process, prior to the actual foreclosure auction. However, she lost her home, her credit, and the thousands of dollars that she invested in the house. On top of that, she still has to pay the lender if the house sold for less than the remaining balance of her loan and she didn't get anything out of the deal.

Linda's situation is an example of the actual foreclosure process in Texas. The foreclosure process varies from state to state, but the options are generally the same from lender to lender. This manual will teach you how to save your home from foreclosure in any state.

So be sure to check out my website at http://behindonpayments.com to get recommendations on what to do. Then come back to this workbook to learn how to do it. You can also find details on the site regarding the foreclosure process in various states.

I believe that MOST of us want to keep our homes, but if foreclosure is inescapable, you'll also learn how to walk away without losing everything like I did.

THE STRATEGY

With all of that said… What's Your 20? Where are you in the foreclosure process?

 HAVE YOU RECEIVED THE FIRST LETTER?

The first letter, often called a "Notice of Default", is informing you that the foreclosure process has begun. In essence, the clock has started, and you now have **41-days** to find a solution. Until you receive this document your house is not in foreclosure. You may receive threatening letters from the lender, notices of penalties, back payments and interest. However, your house is not in foreclosure until you receive a copy of the Notice of Default that has been recorded at the county clerk's office.

 HAVE YOU RECEIVED THE SECOND LETTER?

This letter is the lender's last attempt to contact you prior to selling your house at the foreclosure auction. You now have **21-days** to figure it out.

From the time you receive the first letter up until the hour the house is sold at auction, you have an opportunity to do one of two things - save the house or sell it. You can save your house by coming up with the cash or working with your lender to identify the most profitable resolution. You can also sell the property to any willing buyer as long as the lender agrees with the amount of debt covered by the sale. The following table summarizes the process.

Read your Deed of Trust! It contains strict guidelines regarding the lender's responsibilities. Some Deeds do not require that the first letter be sent if the house does not serve as collateral for the loan. You may receive a letter that is a combination of the two (i.e. a Notice of Default and an Intent to Accelerate).

Keep in mind that the lender is on a strict timetable also. Failure to notify you promptly is grounds for stopping the entire process and starting over- thus giving you more time to come up with the funds. If you do not understand the documents, request that an attorney explain them to you.

Use the diagram below as a quick reference to help you make decisions. It includes the timeline discussed above, as well as the options that are available.

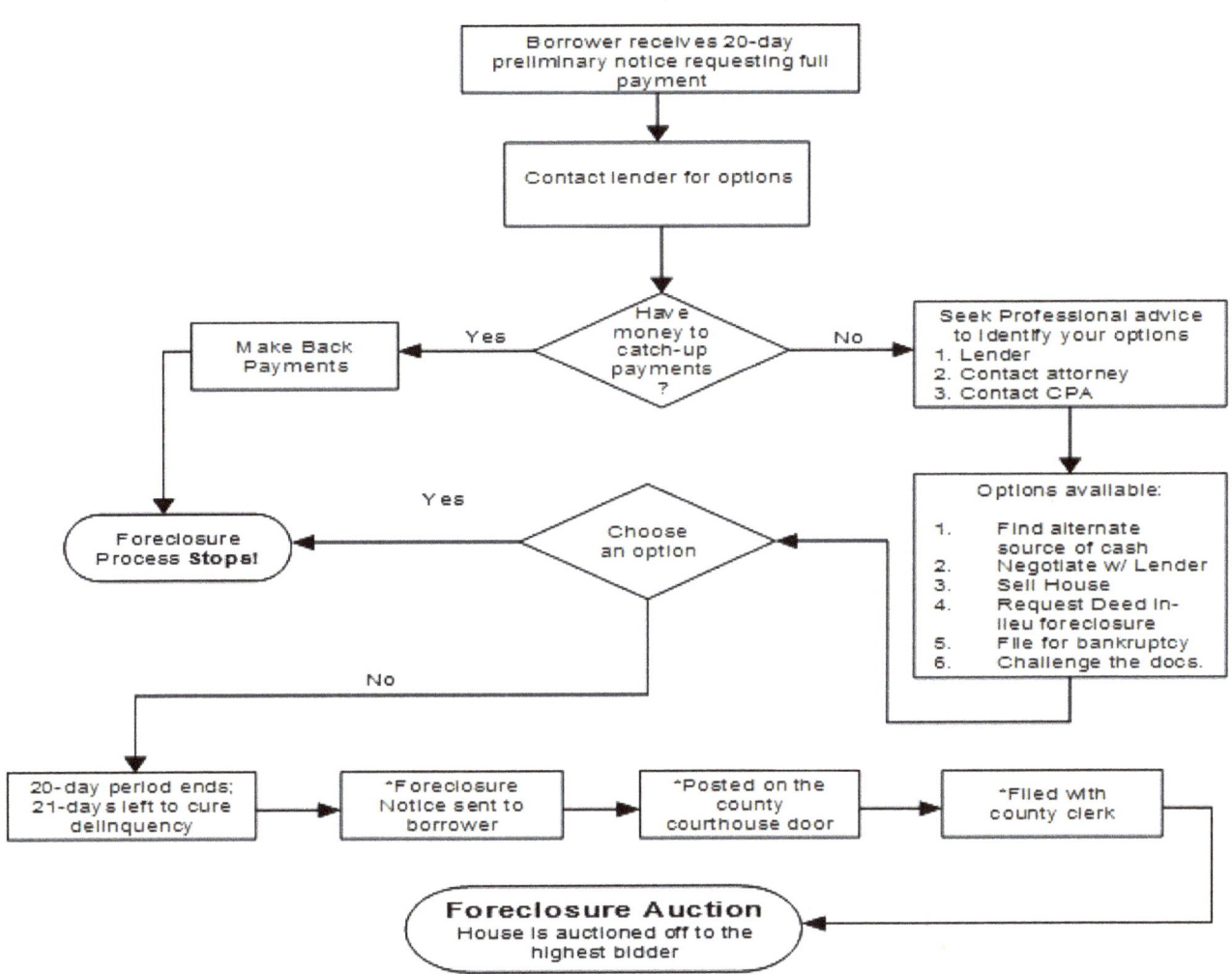

*Note: These items are performed simultaneously.

LENDER ACTIONS THAT COULD STOP OR DELAY FORECLOSURE

Lenders are required to strictly comply with the rules. That includes state and federally mandated laws and acts, as well as guidelines spelled out in the deed of trust. There are certain circumstances that could go wrong for the lender but right for you, therefore you must be knowledgeable every step of the way.

Learn the Game, Know the Clock, and Act Timely!

Be certain to keep track of the following items and make sure that they occurred in accordance with the rules. Here are a few points to ponder according to Judon Fambrough's article "A Homeowner's Rights Under Foreclosure":

- Did the lender have a valid reason to foreclose (i.e. missed payments)?
- Did the lender furnish a 20-day notice to cure the default via certified mail to your last known address (as specified in the lender's records)?
- Were notices properly posted 21 days prior to the auction?
- Check the date recorded at the county clerk's office?
- The postmark on the notification that was forwarded to your residence?
- Check the date that was stamped on the notification at the courthouse?
- Is the house located in one county or two? If two, then:
- Were notices recorded in each county?
- Were notices posted at each county courthouse?
- Did the notice(s) that were forwarded to your residence clearly state the time, date, county and location in which the auction would be held?
- Did all parties responsible for the mortgage receive notification of the sale? (If a married couple is separated, the lender may be responsible for forwarding a notice to both parties if addresses where provided)
- If the original trustee did not perform the sale, was a substitute trustee appointed in accordance with the guidelines of the deed of trust?
- Does the deed of trust require a resignation from the original trustee?
- Was a 21-day notice supposed to be filed announcing a substitute trustee according to the deed of trust?
- Did the sale occur in the area designated by the Commissioners Court?
- Did the sale take place within three hours of the posted time and date?
- Did the trustee acknowledge and accept all bids after reading the notice?
- Did the trustee bid on his/her own behalf?
- Was the borrower alive at the time of the sale? (The executor of the estate usually has a right to revoke the sale up to four years after the borrowers' death)
- Was the borrower a minor?

- Was the debtor on active military leave?

The intent of this manual is not to provide legal advice; it is to give you something to think about. If you would like to obtain greater detail on how the questions above may be helpful in stopping or delaying the foreclosure of your home, discuss them with your attorney who will advise you on how to proceed.

OPTIONS TO SAVE YOUR HOME

Learn the Clock, Know the Game and Act Timely!

 There are six ways to stop the clock at any time during the process. They are:

1. Negotiate with the lender to extend, delay, or forgive the debt.
   (NOTE: This is your best option)
2. Refinance
3. Sell the House
4. File for bankruptcy
5. Challenge the trust deed (If the documents contain mistakes, the court may demand that the foreclosure procedures cease)
6. Pay all back payments, late fees, penalties, and interest.

Let's begin by discussing the last option, paying all back payments, late fees, penalties, and interest. I know that you are probably saying to yourself, "Duh… if I had the money to pay the darn thing off, I wouldn't be in this predicament." Just take it easy, I'd like to suggest a few options for cash that you may not have considered. Sometimes we overlook opportunities simply because there's so much other stuff going on. We tend to look for the apparent solutions like a raise or bonus at work, or even a huge tax refund check versus looking for the not so obvious way out. Nevertheless, here are a few suggestions.

SOURCES OF CASH

Begin reviewing your local newspaper, classified ads, Greensheet, Thrifty Nickel, and Yellow Pages for people who advertise money to lend on real estate. Place a "Money Wanted" ad in the newspaper. Please note, these people will definitely ask the "What's in it For Me?" question, so be prepared. Depending on your current situation, you can offer to pay a certain amount of interest upon repaying the borrowed funds. Or you can offer to extend an equity position by giving them a percentage of ownership in the property. Be sure that you are able (or will be able) in the near future to completely repay the funds. If not, you are digging a deeper hole and postponing an inevitable outcome.

<u>CREDIT UNION</u>

If you are a member of a credit union, contact them at your earliest convenience, and find out what type of loans they have to offer. If you are not member, become one. In most instances, if you work in a certain industry (i.e. education, postal, etc.) or have a relative that works in the industry, you can join. Credit unions will often make loans directly for property, and those that won't, usually provide personal loans.

Credit unions are nonprofit organizations, therefore interest rates on loans are typically lower than they are at many commercial finance companies and somewhat less than the top banks. Most credit unions lend only a few thousand dollars if the funds are unsecured. Keep in mind that to qualify for an unsecured loan, you must have crystal clear credit. Yet, loans secured by real estate may provide homeowners with access to much more capital.

PERSONAL PROPERTY LOANS

Real property refers to land and the improvements (i.e. houses, roads, fences, pipelines, etc.) on it. Personal property is everything else. Most lenders offer personal property loans. These loans can be acquired by pledging such property as boats, cars, refrigerators, etc. The downside to person property loans is that the interest rates are often exceptionally high.

FIND A ROOMMATE/ AIRBNB

Someone that you know may be in need of a place to stay and is willing to pay rent to reside in an extra bedroom. Though this can be an uncomfortable alternative, realize that the arrangement is only for a specified amount of time (long enough for you to get on your feet). Before deciding to implement this option, calculate the amount of money needed on a monthly basis to enable you to send at least an additional $200 along with your existing mortgage payment. It would be a good idea to contact your lender and negotiate an agreed upon payment, prior to renting a room.

BECOME AN ENTREPRENEUR

If you have a skill or talent that you have not tapped into because of a lack of time, begin clearing your schedule now! It's do or die time. If you fix cars on the side, are a handyman, can provide lawn care services or a household cleaning service, make jewelry, or can do anything that does not require a large capital investment, begin doing it to supplement your income. It can be as easy as you make it, so stop making excuses. Create a simple flyer on regular white paper and ask a friend or relative who has printer access to create at least 200 flyers. You don't have to start off big with all of the tools of the trade. As long as you can get the job done with a professional appearance, then go for it. So what if it takes you a tad bit longer without that tool? Do it or figure out a way to gain access to the tool. Notice, I didn't tell you to buy the tool, I said gain access. Maybe you have friends or relatives that will lend it to you. If not, ask them to lease it to you for a small fee. Whatever you have to do, do it. Be creative and make it happen.

When you consider all other options, this is one option where you don't have to beg anyone to give you anything. You may simply request their assistance with acquiring the necessary materials.

LIQUIDATE ASSETS

Why not have a garage sale! Figure out what you own of value, yet seldom use and sell it by having a garage sale or placing classified ads in the local newspaper. Your personal items as discussed earlier are a great place to begin, but don't stop there. Ask your family and friends to clean out their houses and get rid of unwanted items by donating to your cause. Consider selling furniture, jewelry, clothes, boats, cars - you name it. One man's trash can be another man's treasure.

Exercise the option that renders the most cash. If the use of your personal property as collateral to secure a loan will yield more money than out right selling the item, then get the loan.

RECLAIM DEPOSITS

Some organizations- like electricity, home telephone, cellular phone, secured credit card companies and mortgage companies- require deposits prior to rendering services. These deposits are requested as a means of ensuring that the company has security in the event that you fail to make payments. Often, if you no longer need the service or make several timely payments, these creditors will return the deposit…if you remind them. According to Section 10 of the Real Estate Settlement Procedures Act (RESPA), lenders are required to return funds to borrowers if an excess of $50.00 or more exists within the escrow account. Lenders are mandated to perform an annual escrow account analysis and notify borrowers of the status, including any excess or shortfall relating to the account. Call your lender to identify the status of your escrow account and visit https://www.unclaimed.org/ today. If the link doesn't work Google, "Unclaimed Property+ (name of your state)"

INCOME TAX REFUND

If taxes are withheld from your salary, odds are you will receive a refund. This money can be used as a means of curing your default. Check with a tax consultant to identify your options. Ask if you can file early and get your refund EARLY.

INSURANCE

If you currently have a life insurance policy, contact your insurance agent or provider to find out the cash value of the policy. Certain policies typically build equity over years if monthly payments are submitted. There are two (2) options available for retrieving cash from your policy. You can either withdraw the entire amount vested or borrow against the policy. If you do not desire to liquidate the policy, borrow against it. Keep in mind that you are borrowing your own money that has accrued interest. Therefore, if you decide not to replenish your life insurance policy by paying yourself back, there will be less money disbursed if you pass away.

Another form of insurance to review for savings is Private Mortgage Insurance (PMI). The purchase of PMI is required by most lenders if the borrower does not make a down payment of at least twenty percent (20%) of the home's value upon loan origination and closing. The insurance protects lenders from excessive losses in the event of a borrower's default.

On July 29, 1999, the PMI Act became effective under Section 6 of the Real Estate Settlement Procedures Act (RESPA). This Act enables borrowers to request cancellation of PMI if they meet certain criteria and have at least twenty percent (20%) equity in their home. The equity position is based on the original value of the home, and borrowers must submit a written request to their lender for approval. If your loan was originated before July 29, 1999, contact your lender to obtain information on how to cancel PMI. Visit the following site for more details http://www.hud.gov/offices/hsg/sfh/res/respamor.cfm.

CREDIT CARDS

Several credit cards offer cash advances that range from $100- $100,000. This may be just the key to getting you out of a short-term bind. How many credit cards do you have, and how much money can you borrow from each? If you do not have a credit card or you would like to apply for additional cards, there is a terrific website that provides options for possibly every kind of applicant. If you have filed for bankruptcy within the last seven (7) years, or you have missed three (3) or more consecutive payments in the last three years, and even if you currently have credit cards with less than 50% of the credit line available, there may be something for you. The website is www.creditcards.com

Several credit card companies offer programs that allow consumers to defer payments when they experience financial difficulties. Call them to discuss your options and find out if there are penalties for exercising this option. Possible penalties may be:

- An increased interest rate
- A lump sum finance charge
- Or damaging marks against your credit

PAYPAL

PayPal offers personal lines of credit that range from $250-$10,000. This should only be used as short-term option because the interest rate is 25.99%; which is high.

GOOGLE

The place for getting up-to-date information on almost everything! Google, "best personal loans for bad credit + (the current year)."

RETIREMENT FUND

Two options exist regarding your 401(k) depending upon your plan. You can either borrow against your account or completely withdraw all of the money that has accumulated (minus taxes, fees and penalties). Borrowing funds from a 401K is similar to borrowing against a life insurance policy. You simply borrow the money based on prescribed terms and conditions and pay it back on a set schedule. The maximum amount that you can borrow according to Federal Law is the lesser amount of $50,000 or half of your total contribution to the account. The law also stipulates that you can only borrow the funds for a maximum period of five (5) years, and you must pay interest rates according to the current market rate.

Liquidating your account without the intent to repay is where penalties usually apply. The penalties are put in place to strongly discourage you from withdrawing the funds unless you are facing an urgent and severe financial hardship, as defined by IRS Guidelines. Eviction and foreclosure of your primary residence generally meet these guidelines. Be mindful that most plans typically require that you expend all other options, including borrowing from the 401(k), prior to withdrawing the money. The penalties for early withdrawal may include:

- A 10% early withdrawal fee
- A 20% mandatory federal income tax withholding
- The inability to contribute for six months

If your plan allows withdrawals, they may request that you provide proof of your hardship and proof that you have attempted to acquire the funds by other means. You can normally withdraw all of the money that you have contributed to the account, yet you will not receive your employer's contribution or accumulated earnings.

REFINANCE WITH A CO-MORTGAGOR

A co-mortgagor is a person who agrees to be personally responsible for repayment of your mortgage. Now, at this point you're probably saying, "Yeah, right. Why would someone want to do that?" The answer is that a lot of people will be interested if you make the offer sweet enough. For instance, say that you have a friend or relative or investor (see page 39) that is in need of a place to live. This person has a job, good credit, other assets, and can qualify for a loan if need be. The agreement will work as follows:

You and the co-mortgagor enter into a legal agreement that specifies that the individual will be personally liable for the repayment of the mortgage given that you agree to continue making payments on the existing loan. However, in the event that you fail to make even one payment, you'll sign the deed over to them and they will own the house.

Now let me EMPHASIZE that this is a LEGAL AGREEMENT. You have to view it as a business arrangement and be prepared to honor your end of the deal if you miss a payment. My recommendation is that you speak to a volunteer attorney (see Page 80) before signing anything that you don't totally understand.

As you can see, this option is only viable if you are absolutely sure that you are able to make payments from here on out. If you cannot, you may lose your property.

The scenario above may not be suitable for you, however continue to review all options and be creative. See, the key to resolving your present situation is to remain open-minded and continue brainstorming until you reach an answer that fits your needs. Don't give up! Continue to Press On.

BILL DEFERRMENT

A number of creditors will allow you to defer payments for a limited time in order to assist you during times of difficulty. Some bills that may qualify include utilities, phone, student loans, SBA loans, credit cards (as previously mentioned), mortgage, and possibly many others. Call your creditors today to find out if they have such programs.

FRIENDS AND RELATIVES

If this is a sensitive issue for you -which it is for most people- use this option as a last resort, but do not allow your pride to hinder you from asking. Just be sure that you do what you say that you will do. If you say that you'll pay them back, then do it. When you request the funds explain to them how you'll repay (just to give them a sense of security).

CONTEST PROPERTY TAXES

It seems as though property taxes, like unchecked weeds, can absolutely grow out of control if you fail to pay attention to them. From subdivision to subdivision and even house-to-house, wide variances can exist between similar properties on the same block. If you research the average taxes paid in your neighborhood (see How to Use Your County Appraisal District as a Research tool on Page 42-46) and find that you are paying more than those around you with similar properties, then protest. The appraisal district board systematically raises property taxes throughout subdivisions based on sales information within the Multiple Listing Service (MLS) database and the price per square foot calculation. The board uses this calculation to approximate the value of each property. What you can do is challenge the evaluation process by comparing the sales information that they are using to your property, your property condition, and back it up with a lot of documentation. Digital photos of all of the properties will always help your case. The Appraisal District will furnish you with recent comparable sales if you just call them or go by their office prior to your hearing. They will give you the exact information they will use against you in your meeting. Harris County Appraisal District's address is 2800 North Loop West, and the phone number is 713-812-5800.

Take pictures of your house and the surrounding area to prove that repairs are needed (lower valuation) and show such things as the close proximity (across the street) to noisy elementary schools, soccer fields, a Stop N Go, a major street, a run-down commercial project, or near a Section 8 apartment, etc. Even a driveway in need of repair (broken or cracked) may be able to help you out.

Take pictures with you to the meeting to help you win your case.

Knowing the comparable home sales. The comps should have settled in the last 6 months, and be in the same neighborhood, of similar size, style, condition, etc. Email me at support@BehindOnMortgagePayments.com to provide a list of comparable properties in your area.

Be prepared.

If you do not agree with the outcome of the individual who meets with you, you can request an appeal and go before the board.

If it is a rental property, and you are asked the rental amount (which is not the board's business), you should give an amount that is favorable to your case.

🟢 GO <u>Please Protest Your Property Taxes, because contesting property taxes can be one method of decreasing your annual expenses</u>. This two-hour process per year can save you thousands of dollars every year!

The important thing to remember about implementing options that suggest borrowing money at high interest rates is that those options should be viewed as a short-term solution. If not, you'll end up deeper in the hole. Before borrowing, figure out how you plan to pay the money back and over what time period.

🟡 WAIT Only utilize these suggestions if you are sure that you will be able to repay the money borrowed. Several of the alternatives above are time dependent. That is why knowing the clock is so important. **Foreclosure auctions in Texas occur every first Tuesday of the month.** If a couple of days remain before this date, then you may not be able to utilize some the options above so have a backup plan.

For sure, place an ad in the newspaper, and hopefully someone will purchase the home just in time. Take a part-time job or become an entrepreneur and try to raise enough money to stop the clock.

Work as hard as you possibly can and do all that you can humanly do. But just in case you are not able to raise enough money, begin looking for someone to purchase the house. It is best to put the house on the market, at least one month prior to the auction. Just as a Plan B, thus if all else fails you still have one option that will relieve you of the debt and prevent a foreclosure from being posted on your credit. Before you sign any documents to convey ownership of your property, consult with a volunteer real estate attorney and request that a clause be inserted stating that if you are able to acquire the funds at least one week prior to the auction, you can back out of the contract without incurring fines or penalties. Realize that in order to close quickly, title must be run on the property to ensure that no fines, liens or encumbrances exist. This process can take at least two weeks. So be prepared to pay for the title if this clause is included.

🟢 GO Often when we find ourselves in this type of situation, it is very hard to think clearly. I was in a total brain fog. **Therefore, I strongly advise you to ask someone who you trust with your LIFE to help you with this process.** Give them this book as a guide, seek professional assistance from a counseling agency, a realtor, or an attorney prior to making any concrete decisions.

SOCIAL ORGANIZATIONS

The United Way provides funds to various social organizations like churches and county social service offices that are to be distributed to the community in order to assist homeowners and renters who are experiencing tough times. A few of the services that they offer are rent, mortgage and utilities assistance. Receipt of funding from one organization does not disqualify you from receiving funds from other affiliate organizations. Assistance may range from $50.00 to one mortgage payment and is based on availability. A list of organizations that have received funding is provided on Page 77 within the Appendix. Some of these organizations will want to ensure that your lender will indeed accept the funds as a means of stopping foreclosure. The last thing that they would want to do is to provide funds if the house will still be sold at the foreclosure auction.

DEBT CONSOLIDATION

(http://debtconsolidationconnection.com/debtconsolidation.html)

Debt Consolidation can be extremely helpful in lowering interest payments, reducing your overall monthly payments (often by fifty percent (50%) or more), and ultimately improving your credit rating. If you have an average unsecured debt (credit cards, gas cards, signature loans, medical bills, utility bills, etc.) of at least $5000, then a debt consolidation program may start you on the road to financial stability.

Here's how most of these programs work. The agency that you employ will contact your creditors to negotiate lower payments and more favorable terms. Some creditors will reduce or waive future interest charges if their minimum payment requirements are met. They will then take that information and consolidate all of your payments into one fixed rate monthly payment. Each month you forward a payment to the agency, and they distribute the funds to your creditors. No new loan is required!

DEBT CONSOLIDATION LOANS

Debt Consolidation Loans can be used to consolidate both secured (asset used as collateral) and unsecured debt into one monthly payment. The benefit to this option is that interest payments may be tax deductible if your house is used to secure the loan. This type of loan is called a home equity loan. One of the usual stipulations is that you must borrow a lump sum and pay interest on the full amount.

Another alternative is to obtain a home equity line of credit. The difference between a home equity loan and a home equity line of credit is that borrowers can extract funds as needed with the line of credit, versus borrowing a lump sum amount.

An added benefit is that interest rates for home equity loans and home equity lines of credit are usually much lower than conventional loans, so you could save thousands of dollars annually in interest payments alone.

Contact a tax consultant to find out if this option would work for you.

Now consider all of the previous suggestions and write down all potential sources of cash that may help you save your home from default. After writing the amount and the date that the funds will be available, rank them according to the sources that will provide the most amount of money the fastest.

Source of Cash	Amount	Date Funds Available	Ranking
Ex: Sell the Boat	$10,000.00	01/04/04	1
_____	$_____	_____	____
_____	$_____	_____	____
_____	$_____	_____	____
_____	$_____	_____	____
_____	$_____	_____	____
_____	$_____	_____	____
_____	$_____	_____	____
_____	$_____	_____	____
_____	$_____	_____	____
_____	$_____	_____	____
_____	$_____	_____	____
_____	$_____	_____	____
_____	$_____	_____	____
_____	$_____	_____	____
_____	$_____	_____	____
_____	$_____	_____	____
_____	$_____	_____	____
_____	$_____	_____	____
_____	$_____	_____	____
_____	$_____	_____	____
Total	$_____	_____	____

LENDER RELATED FORECLOSURE OPTIONS

Most lenders would rather develop a win-win solution with the borrower than to obtain the home via foreclosure. This is because financial institutions are in the business of lending funds, not acquiring real estate. There are several costs incurred by the lender both before (i.e. legal fees) and after foreclosing (i.e. home repair, sales costs, etc.). Lenders do not foreclose in order to make money, but only reluctantly as a way of limiting losses on a defaulted loan. This is why, if you get behind on your mortgage payments, your lender will work with you to devise a practical plan to cure the default and bring the loan current. In order to do so however, you must maintain communication with your lender and be honest when evaluating your financial situation. To facilitate making an informed decision on which option best suits your needs, you need to identify what options are available. Then you will be in a stronger position when negotiating with the lender's loss mitigation department. Your lender may be able to offer some of the following options:

FORBEARANCE

Special Forbearance is one of the least costly and most effective workout alternatives. It is a formal, written agreement to reduce or postpone a mortgagor's monthly payments for a specified time. The agreement should clearly state:

- The period of reduced or suspended payment
- The schedule for making additional payments when the mortgagor resumes regular monthly payments
- The terms and requirements for paying off the mortgage
- and the date on which the forbearance will end

This option should be sought if you are experiencing a temporary loss or reduction in income and foresee being able to resume regular payments, as well as an additional payment to cure the delinquency after the forbearance period is complete. In most cases the length of the plan will not exceed 18 months from the first reduced or suspended payment and will stipulate commencement of foreclosure action if you default on the agreement. Also keep in mind that your lender may require that at least 25% of the delinquent amount be paid prior to granting this option. Special Forbearance should be considered if the following circumstances apply:

- The death of the Mortgagor or a family member who considerably contributed toward the monthly payment
- Unexpected job loss or source of income
- Sudden increase in living expenses
- Illness or some natural disaster that the Mortgagor was not insured against;
- A non-preventable reduction in income that substantially altered the Mortgagor's ability to perform as agreed

- Other unusual circumstances that are well documented and merit the use of a relief provision (for example, individuals who are affected by a call-up of reservists, yet do not qualify for the Soldiers' and Sailors' Relief Act)

You may also qualify for Special Forbearance if you desire to sell your property as a means of avoiding foreclosure. Most lenders will grant this option during the listing period if there is a large amount of equity in the home. Their decision is usually based on the anticipated length of time required to complete the sale, your ability to pay a portion of the regular monthly payment during the forbearance period, the value of the home, and the length of the forbearance period.

There are additional forbearance options open to select groups of borrowers. For instance, if you are on active duty in the armed forces, if you work for the airline industry, or if you have an FHA loan you may qualify for special provisions within the guidelines of a regular forbearance.

TEMPORARY INDULGENCE

Temporary Indulgence means that the lender will grant a 30-day grace period to allow you to repay the total delinquent amount in one installment. Lenders are willing to grant this option if you can prove that you will be financially able to bring the account completely current within 30 days.

How could you possibly be able to bring the account current in 30 days you ask? Well here's how:

- If you sell or rent the house, and will close within the 30-day window;
- If you have a pending lawsuit and with receive a settlement within 30 days;
- If you will receive funds from a social agency in 30 days;
- If an insurance settlement is being negotiated and …. you know the rest
- If you've sent in payments, yet they were lost and need to be located…
- Even if you need time to develop a formalized plan with the lender- within 30 days.

Now one thing to note is that *everything* is negotiable!

SOLDIERS' AND SAILORS' RELIEF ACT OF 1940

Special provisions exist for individuals who are on active duty in the armed forces. One such provision is the Soldiers' and Sailors' Relief Act. During World War II, Congress passed a federal law that gives rights to all military members as they enter active duty. It provides protection from issues relating to rental agreements, security deposits, prepaid rent, eviction, installment contracts, credit card interest rates, automobile leases, mortgage interest rates, mortgage foreclosure, civil judicial proceedings, and income tax payments. Fannie Mae has made special provisions that allow financial institutions to provide mortgage payment assistance during times of financial difficulty. The Act does not wipe out your obligation to make payments, yet it temporarily suspends the right of creditors to use court action to force them to pay only if their inability to pay is due to military service. After release from active duty, they will be obligated to begin making regular payments within 3-6 months. The Act also stipulates that interest rates can be reduced to six (6%) percent as long as you they on active duty.

Fannie Mae has also temporarily added two (2) additional enhancements to the original Soldiers' and Sailors' Relief Act. The enhancements allow borrowers to provide active duty orders as the only proof of hardship, and military indulgence versus forbearance will be reported to credit bureaus. Ordinarily, borrowers must submit a full range of financial statements and hardship letters as verification of their current financial status. The first enhancement mentioned, saves those on active duty the hassle of creating those documents. The second item mentioned, regarding military indulgence versus forbearance, has been added as a means of credit protection. When creditors see that an individual has requested mortgage forbearance in the past, they wonder if they are *currently* capable of making timely payments or was the request due to chronic financial mismanagement. Military indulgence on the other hand, specifically identifies that the hardship was due to service for our country.

In order to qualify for assistance, Soldier's must currently be on active military duty, or have been on duty within the last three months prior to applying for relief. We reiterate, this Act includes all persons deployed around the world on active duty in the armed forces. Soldiers will also qualify if their mortgage was obtained prior to the date that active duty service began.

Contact a housing counseling agency or an attorney to obtain details.

It is extremely important that you seek legal advice prior to exercising options, to ensure that you choose the option that is most suitable for you.

REPAYMENT PLAN

The development of a Repayment Plan is an ideal option if you have experienced an income-reducing event yet have regained monthly income and are in the process of reestablishing a steady payment history. A repayment plan can be negotiated with your lender, that will allow you to repay an agreed upon portion of the back payments along with your regular monthly payment.

LOAN MODIFICATION

A loan modification involves permanently changing one or more terms of a Mortgage in order to assist the borrower with bringing a delinquent loan current to prevent foreclosure. This option is offered to creditable borrowers as a means of reinstating the loan and modifying the agreement so that the borrower's payments are more manageable. Terms that can be modified include: interest rate reductions at or below the current market rate, conversion of adjustable rate mortgages to fixed-rate mortgages, increase term by the number of months delinquent, or loan re-amortization.

You may qualify for this option if you meet the following guidelines:

- A Mortgagor has experienced a permanent or long-term reduction in income that affects his or her ability to continue making Monthly Payments;

- A Mortgagor granted relief under the Soldiers' and Sailors' Civil Relief Act cannot cure his or her delinquency within three months after being released from active duty;

- The Mortgagor faces legitimate hardship;

- Payments to a retirement account have been suspended and the Mortgagor already has applied funds from retirement accounts or other substantial assets to try to bring the Mortgage current;

- The loan is not a cash-out refinance;

- The Mortgagor's income is less than or equal to his or her expenses prior to the loan modification, and expenses are less than income after modification;

- The terms of the Mortgage Loan (such as those imposed by a nonstandard ARM Loan) contribute toward a greater risk of Default;

- Any other situation in which changing the terms of the Mortgage Loan would cure the present delinquency or avoid foreclosure of the Mortgaged Property or prevent future delinquencies

At this point I'd like to reiterate that ...*everything* is negotiable.

LOAN RESTRUCTURING

Typically, four restructuring options exist. They are interest servicing, tenure extension, full and final settlement and back-end addition.

Interest servicing is when your lender allows you to pay the mortgage interest only for a certain period of time. After the interest only period is complete, you must resume making full payments of interest plus principal. This option is best suited for individuals experiencing momentary difficulty, but who anticipate an increase in income in the near future. If this option is exercised, you run the risk of paying more in interest over the life of the loan. Interest rates in this scenario are also rarely fixed. Therefore, if you exercise this option when interest rates are low, you might end up paying more than planned yet less than if interest rates were in the double digits.

The second option is 'tenure extension'. With this option the length of time granted to fully repay your mortgage is extended, and your monthly payments are reduced. This is another great option if you believe that the reduction in income will be permanent or long-term.

The third option is full and final settlement. If you are on the verge of bankruptcy, communicate that to your lender and watch them squirm. We'll discuss bankruptcy in a moment, however it's very important for you to know that most lenders would rather forgive all (typically if it is less than $5,000.00) or a portion of the debt, than for you to file for bankruptcy. If you offer your lender a one-time lump sum payment of at least 75% of the delinquent amount, they might be willing to accept it as full payment. It doesn't hurt to try. Of course, this option works best if you have a lump sum of money available.

And lastly, if you have at least fifteen (15%) percent equity in your home - negotiable remember- you may be able to restructure the loan by adding the delinquent amount to the loan balance (you may not qualify if you have missed more than six (6) payments). This is one of the easiest options because it allows you to continue making your normal monthly payment, without the struggle of coming up with additional funds to clear the delinquency.

PARTIAL CLAIM

A partial claim is an interest free loan provided by your lender on behalf of HUD in order to repay your delinquency and bring the loan current. If you decide to exercise this option HUD will create a promissory note and subordinate mortgage. You are not responsible for repaying the loan until you pay off the first mortgage or sell the property. This is an excellent option if you are not currently in foreclosure, can begin making full mortgage payments, and your loan is at least four (4) months delinquent (no more than 12 months).

REFINANCING

Refinancing is an alternative method of absorbing the delinquency and/or lowering your monthly payment. If refinancing is an option that will work for you and you have equity in your home, consider withdrawing the equity. Once it is withdrawn, give the entire amount back to the lender and request that the cash be applied to your principal balance. By doing this, you've just made several monthly payments toward your loan, which buys time for you to get on your feet. This is a terrific strategy if you are currently unable to make payments and cannot foresee when you will be able to begin making regular payments again.

Refinancing is generally based on credit scores; therefore, it may be more difficult to qualify for this option if your credit score is below 500 but it definitely doesn't hurt to try. If you do qualify, the lender may forgive a portion of the debt and refinance the remainder with a sub-prime loan. Sub-prime loans are those that have higher interest rates and offer less favorable terms than prime loans (traditional bank loans). This usually results in higher monthly mortgage payments. This could be the answer, if it will help you to save your property. Yet please take into account the cost of saving it. Remember that your payments could increase, depending upon how the terms are structured. To find out if your payments will increase, simply ask the lender.

Recent studies by the Consumers Union and Austin's Tenant's Council-- "Access to the Dream 2000" -- found inequities in the practice of sub-prime refinancing to minority borrowers (African Americans, Hispanics, women, elderly, etc.) in low-income neighborhoods. Sub-prime lenders generally target individuals with less than perfect credit and charge high interest rates. This trend is particularly noticeable in the Houston and Dallas markets.

Another option is to ask your current lender if they provide streamline refinancing. Typically, no credit check or appraisal is required, and the origination fees are less.

As a final alternative, explore refinancing through a "hard money" lender. Hard money is easier to obtain than conventional loans, yet the terms (i.e. interest rates and fees) are often much more stringent. One option is to finance only the delinquent amount with hard money, in order to save the house from foreclosure, and then repay the loan as soon as possible to avoid paying lots of interest. Be sure that you have an exit plan prior to acquiring a loan with expensive fees. Your exit plan may be a tax refund, an employment bonus, or a new job. The point is to know how you'll repay the money prior to getting it.

DEED IN-LIEU OF FORECLOSURE

Deed in-lieu of foreclosure means that you have agreed to deed the house to the lender as a means of satisfying the debt and avoiding foreclosure. This is the best option if the property has been on the market for at least three (3) months and not sold or if you do not qualify for other options. Use it as a last-ditch effort to save your credit and not go bankrupt.

NATURAL DISASTER

Homes affected by natural disaster or catastrophe, are typically protected by government policy or insurance. Therefore, if your home has been affected by a catastrophe or natural disaster such as hurricane, tornado, flood, wildfire, earthquake, or other natural or man-made event, and the area has been declared a disaster area by the President of the United States, more than likely your lender will not start the foreclosure process for at least ninety (90) days. Contact your lender immediately to inform them that you are an affected borrower, either physically or financially, and be prepared to provide supporting documentation so that the lender can determine if you meet the relief criteria. Once identified as an affected borrower, foreclosure action may be stopped, or late fees waived for the duration of the moratorium period.

FHA loans are generally covered by a foreclosure moratorium that will automatically stop all foreclosure actions against families with delinquent loans on homes within the boundaries of disaster areas once lenders are notified. If you possess a VA or Conventional loan, contact your lender for qualification, knowing that most lenders abide by FHA's policy to make every effort not to foreclose on properties that have been affected by these unforeseen events.

Some of the actions that your lender may take are:

- During the term of the suspension, your loan may not be referred to foreclosure.

- Your lender will provide all available loss mitigation assistance to help you retain your home.

- Your lender may enter into other options mentioned within this text, such as: a special forbearance plan, loan modification, or partial claim.

With all of the options mentioned above, keep the following tips in mind:

Your lender will decide which options you qualify for based on your individual circumstances and ability to abide by a modified arrangement.

If your income is limited, so are the options that are available to you. Prepare.

If you can, continue making mortgage payments until a new arrangement is approved. That is why I recommend that you contact your lender as soon as an event occurs that will affect your ability to pay your mortgage.

If you cannot continue making FULL payments, save what can in case they request that you pay a portion upfront. If you absolutely can't make a payment or save partial payments, keep in mind that they can put the arrearage at the back end of the loan. But you have to show that you can afford to

A new mortgage, loan modification or other arrangement is not a guarantee against foreclosure if you fail to meet the terms of your new or modified mortgage.

If saving your home is not feasible due to permanent income modifications, lenders may suggest a short sale or a deed-in-lieu of foreclosure, which will be discussed in the next chapter. Just keep in mind that if all else fails, be prepared to cut your losses and regroup…Here's how…

HOW TO KNOW WHEN IT IS TIME TO SELL YOUR HOUSE

Here is my honest advice:

- If you have lost a major source of income that was used to pay your mortgage and can no longer pay the full payment amount, AND
- You do not have a definite date for when that income will be replaced, AND
- You have missed two (2) mortgage payments

Then you should begin the process of selling your house.

I say the 2nd missed payment because in some states (like Texas) the foreclosure process *can* begin after the 3rd missed payment.

Do not wait until you start receiving Notices of Default from your lender.

Because at that point the foreclosure process has begun, and your time is limited.

Limited time often mean less money in your pocket!

Always put yourself in the best situation to recover…sometimes lowering your monthly bills is necessary

Copy this phrase into Google to find out how many payments you can miss before foreclosure starts in your state: "How many payments can I miss in (the name of your state) before my house goes into foreclosure."

WHEN SHOULD YOU TAKE ACTION?

As soon as you see that you that you will not have the money, and will miss your 2nd mortgage payment, take action!

Let me continue by saying that I believe in "God/ a Higher Being."

I practice the Laws of the Universe.

I meditate.

I believe that miracles are possible and occur every day.

With that being said… I also believe that individual action and preparation are necessary.

Expect the best; yet prepare for all possible scenarios.

If you do not take Action…

You will lose your home without making a dime from the equity that you've accumulated!

TAKE THE FOLLOWING ACTIONS IMMEDIATELY!

1) Visit BehindonMortgagePayments.com
2) Complete the four (4) questions
3) Print out the four (4) recommendations provided
4) Then return to this section and continue reading. Details on how to perform each action is provided below.

HOW TO SHORT SELL YOUR HOUSE FOR MAXIMUM PROFIT

The object here is to be able to pay off a negotiated amount of the mortgage debt, fees and expenses; walk away without a foreclosure or bankruptcy on your credit; put a little cash in your pocket to start over; and have the buyer pay all the closing costs. Even if the proceeds of the sale are less than the delinquent amount, many lenders often agree to accept the sale as total satisfaction of your mortgage obligation. That type of arrangement is called a short sale

To qualify for this option, you must be at least two months behind on mortgage payments and prove that you are facing a hardship (job loss, chronic illness, divorce, etc.) that prevents you from making payments.

The "as is" appraised value and the sales price should be least 70-80% of the unpaid principal balance of the home. You must also be able to close on the sell no later than one (1) to two (2) months after the auction. (Note: These percentages are not a hard and fast standard for all lenders, but they are a starting point.)

For example, if you owe $180,000 on your existing home loan, then the house must presently appraise for a minimum of $144,000.

Example Calculation: Your Calculation:

$180,000   Loan Balance: $_____
x   0.80   x 0.80
$144,000   Min. Appraisal: $_____

The house can then be sold for a minimum of $144,000 (which is 80% of the appraised value), although selling the house for $180,000 would be more favorable.

There are a couple of ways to sell your home, yet all options are **time dependent**. That is why knowing where you are in the process is critical. So, at what point is it best to sell the house?

It's a good idea to try to sell your house *as a backup plan* from the moment you figure out that you don't know how you'll make your mortgage payments to one (1) month before the foreclosure auction. Why one month before the foreclosure auction? Because it takes at least two (2) weeks to obtain title insurance, and (if all paperwork is provided to the lender at least) another two (2) weeks to process loan paperwork *unless* you have a cash buyer.

Remember the phrase "backup plan". Contracts can be written in your favor, so speak to a volunteer attorney (see Page 79) about including the following items:

- If you acquire the funds to repay the default at any time before the foreclosure auction, then the contract is void
- If you work out arrangements with your lender to keep the house at any time before the foreclosure auction, then the contract is void
- The property will be sold as is
- Closing will not occur prior to one day before the foreclosure auction

LOCATING BUYERS

Let's talk about locating buyers. The two effective methods for quickly locating buyers are to list the house with a real estate agent or contact an association of real estate investors. You can also sell the house yourself by placing ads in local newspapers. This option may require more time; therefore, we'll only discuss the first two (2) options in detail.

LOCATING A REALTOR

The conventional method of locating buyers is to contact a Real Estate Agent and ask them to list your property. In order to locate a realtor, review the Yellow Pages or request referrals from friends. If you contact an agent, they will come out to evaluate your home and more than likely request that you sign a document that allows them to represent you when speaking to perspective buyers. Remember, DO NOT LET ANYONE PRESSURE YOU INTO SIGNING ANYTHING. After evaluating your property, the agent will run what's called a market analysis to identify what price houses with similar square footage, number of bedrooms/bathrooms, and features have sold for within one (1) mile of your neighborhood in the last six (6) to twelve (12) months. The agent will then suggest a list price that you can either accept or reject. Once your property is listed in the Multiple Listing Service (MLS), it will be available to all agents (thus potential buyers) in your area.

Disadvantages

Though the agent handles all of the details, they do not do it for free. Agents usually charge between two (2%) to six (6%) percent of the final negotiated sales price. The seller (that's you) customarily pays for fees associated with both the buyers' and sellers' agent (which usually totals 6%). If you have negotiated a short sale with your lender, then the lender has accounted for closing cost within the approved price. That mean that you will not have any out of pocket costs at closing.

Another disadvantage is that most buyers that are looking to reside in a property, want the house to look brand new. Therefore, you must take into account the cost to repair your property prior to listing it. Or, if enough equity exists, be prepared to reimburse the seller for requested repairs after closing. **Please note, you do not have to perform repairs. You can sell the house as-is**. But if your house is not in tip-top condition, then you will not get full market value.

Advantages

The number one advantage to listing your house with an agent is that you may be able to obtain full market value for your home. Again, this is time dependent, so if you have lots of time you can request more money. The coverage that the listing obtains is also a huge advantage. Another advantage is that the agent walks you through the entire process. As a result, you do not have to search for prospective buyers, negotiate the price and terms of sale directly, or even know the entire sales process. The agent will handle all of the details and walk you step-by-step through the process.

LOCATING AN INVESTOR

An alternative to listing your house with a realtor is to locate an investor that is willing to purchase your home. This is the best option if you must sell the house quickly, because they are often able to close in as little as 10 days. Investors are also very helpful with developing creative solutions so that you can sell your house with no out-of-pocket expenses, thus you can walk away scot-free. If requested, they may provide guidance on how you can save your home as well.

BehindonMortgagePayments.com is part of a real estate network and has access to many investors and agents. We may be able to assist you with finding an honest agent or investor that is willing to work with you in creating a win-win situation in your area. Email us at support@BehindOnMortgagePayments.com or call (713) 903-7107 to get started.

You can also take matters into your own hands by locating an investor on your own. In order to locate an investor review Craig's List, Google, your local newspaper or Yellow Pages. Their ads usually state "I Buy Houses" or "Cash for Houses", so they are pretty easy to recognize. Another great way to find multiple investors is to contact your local real estate investment club. Visit the following link in order to obtain a list of investment clubs throughout the nation: http://www.creonline.com/real-estate-clubs/index.html. Ask if they can refer you to someone who may be interested in purchasing your property. If you have time, it may also be a good idea to pass out flyers at their monthly meeting.

Disadvantages

The disadvantage of working with investors is that they purchase houses in order to make money by performing repairs and reselling the house or renting it out. In order to make money, they must obtain the house at a discounted rate (usually 30-50% below market value). That means that you will not walk away with all of your equity. So, prior to making the decision to sell to anyone for less than the full amount, consider what you stand to gain and what you stand to lose. Also, watch out for scammers. Certain people will try to prey on your lack of knowledge so take heed to the useful tips on Pages 71-72.

Advantages

The advantage to working with an investor is that they can move very quickly. Plus, you will not have to perform repairs, make back payments, pay foreclosure attorneys, pay a reinstatement fee, or pay late fees. You can walk away with a portion of your equity in order to start over (depending on the number of repairs needed and how long you have to shop investors for the best offer), no foreclosure or bankruptcy on your credit, and hopefully less stress. Remember what I said at the beginning of the workbook, this is a temporary situation. Just make sure that you walk away with all that you can, and don't allow anyone to push you around. The key is to educate yourself as much as possible…so you're already on the right track.

YOUR HOME'S MARKET VALUE

Realtors and investors can be quite sophisticated. They often know more about your home than you do because a great deal of information can be found on the internet. They have access to such information as the value of your home, the square footage, the number of bedrooms and bathrooms, what similar houses in the neighborhood have sold for, and if the owner on record is current on taxes. Most of this information can be obtained by visiting http://www.hcad.org/Records for homes in Harris County or http://www.txcountydata.com for all other Texas counties. For counties in other states, go to Google.com and type "(the name of your county) + appraisal district".

The very best advice that I can give, is for you to do your homework prior to calling a realtor or investor.

Know the value of your home. Contact a realtor and request a market analysis or visit the following websites:

- http://www.har.com/indexrecenthomesales.cfm?clickid=solddata
- http://www.courthousedirect.com/ (Nationwide Information)
- http://taxcountydata.com (for all other Counties)

- http://www.hcad.org
- http://zillow.com
- http://www.eppraisal.com/
- https://www.remax.com/homevalues/houston-tx-p001.html?query=addr-1715%20moritz%20dr%2011,%20houston,%20tx
- https://www.forsalebyowner.com/sell-my-house/pricingscout/landing/

Know the cost of all necessary repairs. Obtain at least three quotes and be willing to provide information regarding the lowest repair quote to the buyer upon request.

Lastly, figure out your bottom-line position. Use the following formula as a starting point:
Market Value – Repairs - Closing Costs = List Price

If there is not much time (i.e. less than or equal to two weeks remaining) before the auction, sell to an investor. If you have at least one and a half (1.5) months to work with, sell to the best offer.

HOW TO DEVELOP A BOTTOM-LINE SELLING POSITION

Now let's discuss how to develop a bottom-line position based on the following formula, concentrating specifically on how to estimate the market value and closing costs:

Market Value – Repairs - Closing Costs = List Price

MARKET ANALYSIS

Market Analysis involves comparing your house to houses with:

- Similar square footage, number of bedrooms/bathrooms
- Similar features (fireplace, pool, waterfront, etc.)
- Within one (1) mile of your home
- Year Built
- And sold within the last six (6) to twelve (12) months

- As previously mentioned, the following websites can be used to determine the value of your home: http://www.eppraisal.com/ or http://www.zillow.com/.

For best results, enter only the name of your street or surrounding streets as an address. These sites will tell you what houses in your area have sold for. Compare your house to houses with similar characteristics and you'll have a ballpark sales price.

Another method of obtaining a rough estimate of the appraised value of your home is to research the data contained within your county appraisal district's website. Most county appraisal district websites provide information regarding market value, neighborhood sales information, house description, tax information, and much more. **TO FIND THE WEBSITE FOR YOUR COUNTY'S APPRAISAL DISTRICT, GOOGLE "(NAME OF YOUR COUNTY) + APPRAISAL DISTRICT."** For instance, I'm in Harris County so I'd Google "Harris County Appraisal District."

The information that follows will teach you how to navigate through the Harris County Appraisal Districts website step-by-step. Though other county websites may be structured differently, much of the basic information is provided. I suggest that regardless of the county in which you reside, walk through the illustration below so that you will be familiar with the type of data necessary to roughly evaluate the appraisal value of your home. Let's begin....

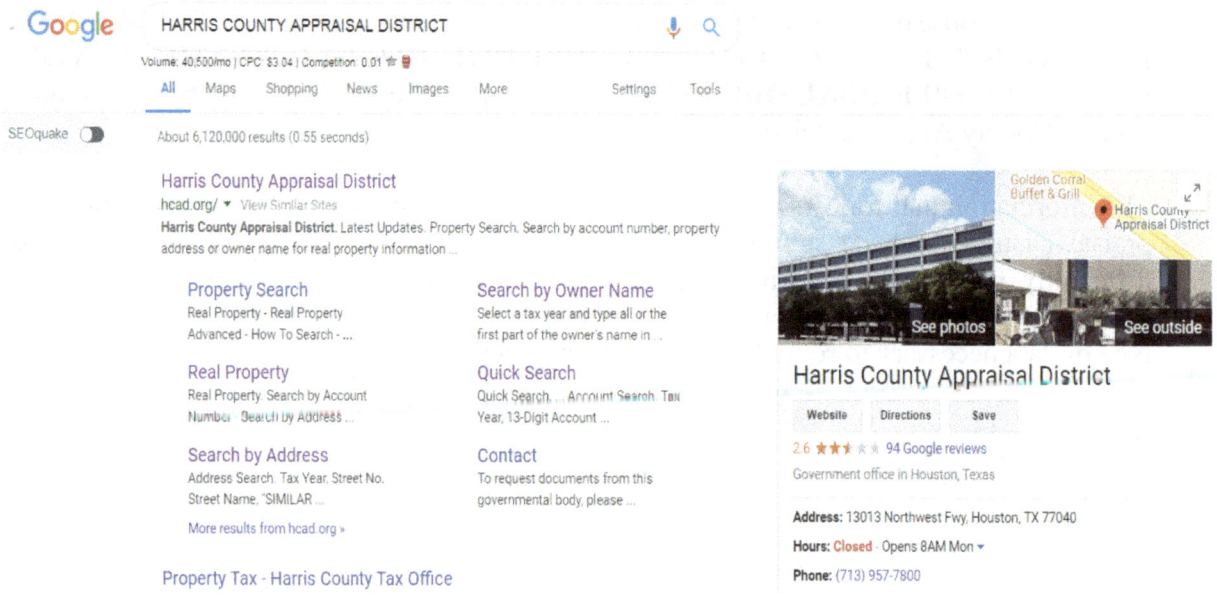

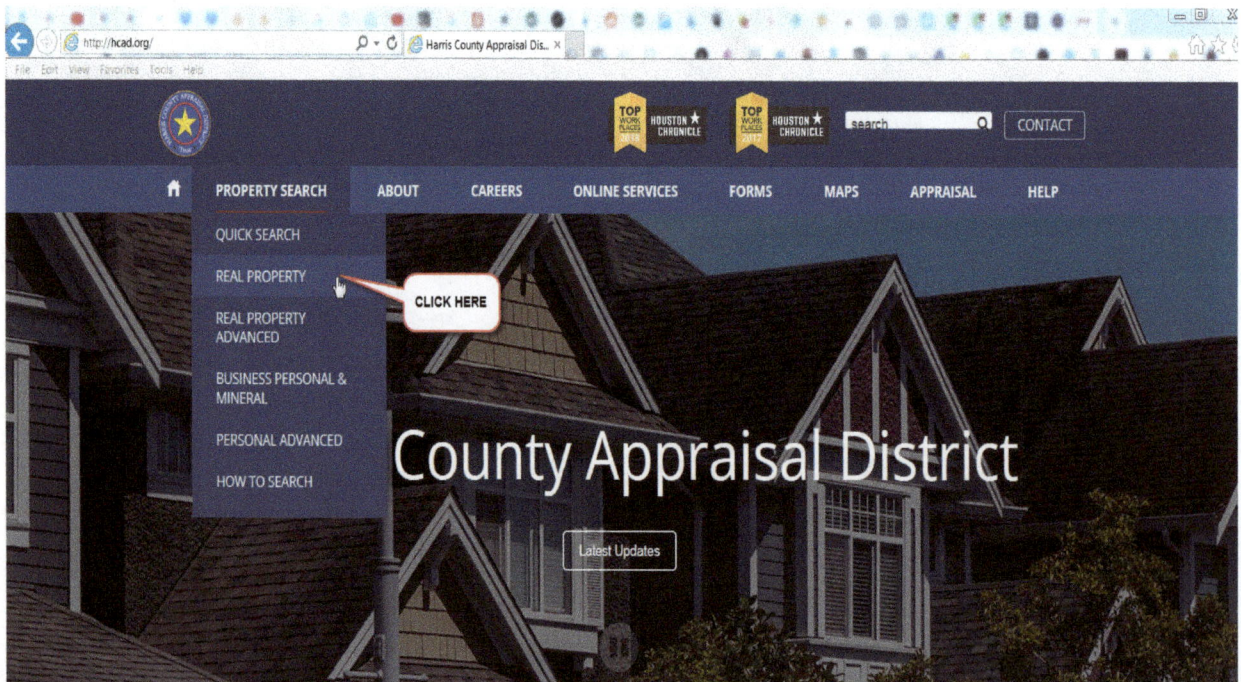

Search using your name, press the Owner Name button then type your last name and first initial into the dialogue box and press enter. Here is a screen shot of the results from a random name search.

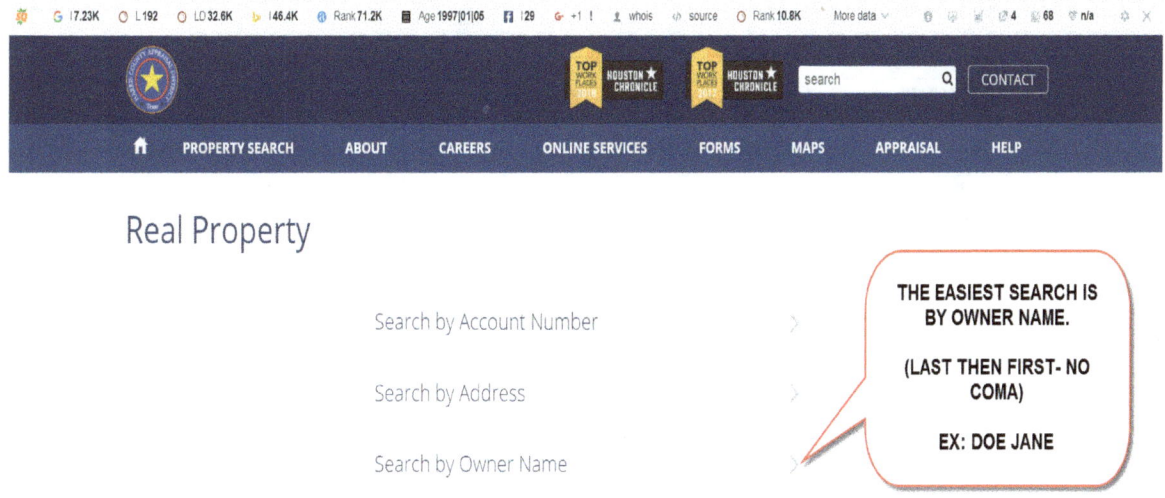

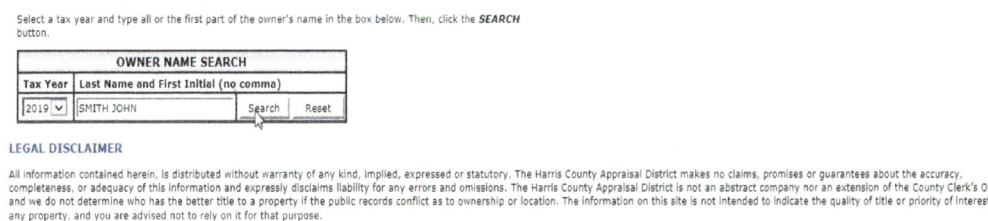

In the event you are unable to retrieve your records using your name, press the address link then type your property address into the dialogue boxes and press enter. If that doesn't work, do a broader search by typing an address range.

		File A Protest	Similar Owner Name	Nearby Addresses	Same Street Name	Related Map 5262C			
				Ownership History					
				Owner and Property Information					
Owner Name & Mailing Address:	CURRENT OWNER CURRENT ADDRESS	**Click Here to Contest Your Property Taxes**		Legal Description: Property Address:	TR 3 OF LT 21 BLK 3 HIGHLAND ACRE HOMES 7539 BRADMAR ST HOUSTON TX 77088		**This tab will show the value of neighboring properties**		
	State Class Code					Land Use Code			
	A1 -- Real, Residential, Single-Family					1001 -- Residential Improved			
Land Area	Total Living Area	Neighborhood	Neighborhood Group		Market Area			Map Facet	Key Map®
5,408 SF	1,192 SF	947	9001		282 -- ISD 09 - Outside Airport Tiers, West of I-45			5262C	412S

		Value Status Information	
Value Status		Notice Date	Shared CAD
Noticed		04/23/2019	No

			Exemptions and Jurisdictions				
Exemption Type	Districts	Jurisdictions		Exemption Value	ARB Status	2018 Rate	2019 Rate	Online Tax Bill
None	009	ALDINE ISD			Not Certified	1.435888		
	040	HARRIS COUNTY			Not Certified	0.418580		
	041	HARRIS CO FLOOD CNTRL			Not Certified	0.028770		
	042	PORT OF HOUSTON AUTHY			Not Certified	0.011550		
	043	HARRIS CO HOSP DIST			Not Certified	0.171080		
	044	HARRIS CO EDUC DEPT			Not Certified	0.005190		
	045	LONE STAR COLLEGE SYS			Not Certified	0.107800		
	061	CITY OF HOUSTON			Not Certified	0.588310		

Texas law prohibits us from displaying residential photographs, sketches, floor plans, or information indicating the age of a property owner on our website. You can inspect this information or get a copy at HCAD's information center at 13013 NW Freeway.

		Valuations		**This is the appraised value according to HCAD**	
Value as of January 1, 2018			Value as of January 1		
	Market	Appraised		Market	Appraised
Land	13,304		Land	18,293	
Improvement	61,290		Improvement	58,360	
Total	74,594	74,594	Total	76,653	76,653
		5-Year Value History			

The values listed for houses on the same street will give you an idea of what your house will sell for (note: there are several other factors that influence this value like property condition, physical dimensions, features (pool, chimney) etc.). The appraised values calculated by HCAD are generally 3% below the values calculated by professional appraisers because HCAD performs the appraisal from a distance, which is called a desk appraisal. Professional appraisers actually enter into the property, so their appraisals are more detailed and complete.

If you'd like to obtain more accurate information than that provided by your appraisal district, contact a local realtor and they can perform a market analysis for you (generally at no cost) or a certified appraiser. The realtor may try to convince you to sign a contract for them to list the property, however you are not obligated to do so unless you feel that it is in your best interest.

CLOSING COSTS

Closing costs are the collection of fees that are associated with buying or selling a home. Everything is negotiable; however, some costs are dictated by local custom while others are automatically allocated to either the buyer or seller. The seller's primary responsibility at closing is to satisfy the remaining balance of the mortgage unless the house is paid for. This balance will be verified prior to closing, before proceeds are dispersed to the seller.

So exactly who pays for what? It's short and simple. Request that the buyer pay for everything. Figure out what your closing costs will be prior to providing a sales price to potential buyers. Then include all seller-closing costs in the sales price. If that's not possible, negotiate the fees, item by item.

Keep in mind that taxes are usually paid at the end of the year. Therefore, these costs are typically distributed between buyer and seller, depending upon the time of year the house is sold. For instance, if closing occurs in October then the seller will be responsible for paying taxes for those ten (10) months and the buyer will pay the rest.

The table that follows was created by Bankrate.com and shows a comparison of closing costs in 2017. The information is based on a $200,000 mortgage loan for a borrower who has good credit and is providing a 20% down payment at closing. However, the aim is to give you an idea of nationwide average closing costs so that you can make more informed decisions.

Texas closing costs

BANKRATE.COM   MAY 12, 2017 in MORTGAGES

Dallas closing costs

Loan amount	$200,000
Itemized origination fees charged by the lender	
Origination points	$1,222
Commitment fee	$370
Document preparation	$79
Broker, originator or lender	$865
Processing	$1,195
Tax service	$78
Underwriting	N/A
Itemized third-party fees	
Appraisal	$462
Attorney, closing or settlement	$456
Credit report	$25
Flood certification	$11
Postage/courier	$36
Survey	$425

Taxes

Borrower's share of state and local transfer taxes and fees	$0
Mortgage tax	$0

Origination fees charged by lender	$982
Third-party fee	$1,203
Taxes	$0
Total	$2,186

Houston closing costs

Loan amount	$200,000

Itemized origination fees charged by the lender

Origination points	$1,206
Commitment fee	$370
Document preparation	$79
Broker, originator or lender	$865
Processing	$1,195
Tax service	$81
Underwriting	N/A

Itemized third-party fees

Appraisal	$462
Attorney, closing or settlement	$456
Credit report	$25
Flood certification	$11
Postage/courier	$36
Survey	$425

Taxes

Borrower's share of state and local transfer taxes and fees	$0
Mortgage tax	$0

Origination fees charged by lender	$983
Third-party fee	$1,203
Taxes	$0
Total	$2,186

San Antonio closing costs

Loan amount	$200,000
Itemized origination fees charged by the lender	
Origination points	$1,222
Commitment fee	$370
Document preparation	$79
Broker, originator or lender	$865
Processing	$1,195
Tax service	$78
Underwriting	N/A
Itemized third-party fees	
Appraisal	$462
Attorney, closing or settlement	$456
Credit report	$25
Flood certification	$11
Postage/courier	$36
Survey	$425
Taxes	
Borrower's share of state and local transfer taxes and fees	$0
Mortgage tax	$0
Origination fees charged by lender	$982
Third-party fee	$1,203
Taxes	$0
Total	$2,188

Other costs may include:

- Agent Costs: Which are usually 3%-6% of the sales price.
- Repair Costs: Which are provided by contractors.
- Liens: Which can include work performed on your property yet not paid for in full. To find out if there are liens on your property, go to www.courthousedirect.com. Review the Useful Links section, located in the bottom left corner of the page for instructions on how to use the site.
- Homeowners Dues

Closing Cost Calculator:

https://smartasset.com/mortgage/closing-costs#TQw1ocMDfl

FOR SALE SUMMARY

Option(s)	Description	Purchase Price	Timing	Means of Locating
Agent	Buy/Sell Homes for Others	Possibly Fair Market Value	Depends on Market, Type of Buyer & Financing	Yellow Pages, Local Newspapers and Referrals
Investor	Buy/Sell Homes as personal investment	10-30% Below Market Value	Usually one month or less	Local Newspaper(s), Yellow Pages and Contact Real Estate Investment Clubs
For Sale by Owner (FSBO)	Owner sells home independently	Varies	Depends on Market, Type of Buyer & Financing	Advertise in local newspapers, FSBO magazines and FSBO websites

Be open to suggestions from realtors, bankers and investors yet always keep in mind that if something smells fishy it most likely is. Don't make a final decision without seeking unbiased advice from a professional.

SELLER FINANCING OPTIONS

LOAN ASSUMPTION

Loan assumption can be exercised as an option prior to getting to the point of foreclosure or it can easily compliment a pre-foreclosure sale. It is a method of transferring ownership of your property to a new buyer who agrees to take responsibility for the existing mortgage. The advantages of assumable loans are:

- The buyer does not have to qualify for a new loan
- No lender processing fees, points or VA funding fees (only attorney's fees for drafting a Contract for Deed)
- No credit checks
- Low down payment
- Reduced closing costs
- Faster closing

VA loans that were originated prior to March 1988 and FHA loans originated before December 1, 1989 are fully assumable. Most loans (VA, FHA, Conventional etc.) today are not fully assumable because they include a due-on-sale clause that allows the lender to request full payment of the entire loan if ownership of the mortgaged property is transferred. In some cases, to avoid the cost incurred to foreclose the lender will waive the due on sale clause and allow a delinquent mortgage to be assumed by a creditable buyer.

Lenders may consider an assumption as a viable alternative to foreclosure if the current market value of the property equals or exceeds the unpaid principal balance plus interest and projected sales costs. An Assumption also may be considered when the current market value of the property is slightly less than the outstanding mortgage because a buyer may be willing to assume the outstanding debt because of the lower closing costs. If major repairs are necessary, thus adding to the lender's loss, it may be advantageous for them to waive the due on sale clause and allow a new buyer to assume the loan and repair the property.

CONTRACT FOR DEED

If you do not possess an assumable loan, then a contract for deed may be another alternative. A contract for deed is simply seller financing, where the buyer takes over your existing loan payments. It generally works like this:
- The seller executes a Deed to the buyer at closing which is not recorded
- The buyer then implements a Note to the seller promising to pay off the loan, and pays the down payment and closing costs
- The buyer and seller then implement a Contract for Deed, which states that when the buyer completes payment of the existing loan, title will be transferred into the buyer's name and the Deed will be recorded
- The title attorney records the Contract for Deed at the County Clerk's Office

- The buyer takes possession of the property, and enjoys all rights of ownership (i.e. tax deductions), yet holds an interest in the property versus legal title

The buyer can either forward these payments directly to you (the seller), the escrow agent or the lender. If an escrow agent is not utilized, then both parties should check regularly to ensure that timely payments are being made. I highly recommend that you contact an attorney to ensure that your interests are protected. A Contract for Deed can be complicated.

Advantages

The advantages to the Seller are:

- Faster Closing with reduced costs (no loan processing time)
- No appraisal fees
- The buyers' down payment can cover the amount of default
- Increased number of potential buyers
- The seller can increase the interest rate to the buyer and receive an annual profit. For example: if your interest rate is 7% on a $100,000 loan ($7000 paid in interest/year), then you could charge the buyer 9%. So, the buyer would pay $9000 in interest/year, which gives you an annual $2000 profit!
- No need to file for bankruptcy

Disadvantages

Possible disadvantages are:

You remain responsible for ensuring that loan payments are made because the loan is in your name. Payment to an escrow agent could be a solution.

The lender could call the entire loan balance due according to the due on sale clause if they find out. At which time the buyer would have to refinance or possibly face foreclosure. Violating the due on sale clause is not illegal however it does defy the conditions of the loan. Though lenders have a right to call the loan due, they generally do not do so *if* timely payments are being made. Remember the cost of foreclosure that we spoke about earlier. Foreclosure would cause them to lose more money than they would gain.

Potential buyer default. The good thing about utilizing a contract for deed versus a lease agreement is that the buyer has more to lose (i.e. down payment, closing cost, homeowner's association fees, maintenance, taxes, etc.). To mitigate the possibility of default, behave somewhat like a lender. Request the buyer's W-2's from the last two (2) years, run a credit check and pay an independent underwriter or a mortgage broker to evaluate their credentials.

BANKRUPTCY

As the ultimate last attempt to save yourself from financial ruin, consider filing for bankruptcy. This is not a decision that should be taken lightly or made without legal consultation. Most people are not aware that bankruptcy will not save your house from foreclosure, yet it will buy you more time to get your finances in order. However, if your creditors are granted a "relief from stay", they can proceed with actions to foreclose.

The ramifications of bankruptcy can last anywhere from seven (7) to ten (10) years and make it very difficult to obtain credit. As adults we learn that credit makes the world go around. Without it, we have difficulty obtaining cars, homes, credit cards, and many other material goods. Creditors and lenders rank bankruptcy as the worst condition of personal or business credit upon review. So be certain that you know and understand the consequences that accompany bankruptcy. Again, seek consultation from an attorney that specializes in bankruptcies prior to finalizing your decision.

Okay, with that out of the way, allow me to provide a brief summary of what bankruptcy is and what various forms are available.

Bankruptcy is the legal means by which plans are developed by debtors who are unable to repay creditors. It is generally sought as a means of settling outstanding debts by fairly dividing assets among creditors. In layman's terms, bankruptcy is a way to wipe the slate clean and start over. There is a possibility that certain debts will be discharged without full repayment after all assets are divided.

There are thirteen chapters in the official bankruptcy law book. However, we will discuss the four most commonly sought options, which are chapters 7, 11, 12 and 13.

CHAPTER 7-LIQUIDATION

Chapter 7 is the fastest and least expensive of all bankruptcy alternatives. It is used by approximately 70% of all consumers filing bankruptcy petitions because it generally takes from three (3) to eight (8) months to be discharged from non-exempt debts. It is also most often used by people who are very deep in debt or do not have a steady income. Chapter 7 involves the complete liquidation of assets as a means of debt satisfaction and can be filed only once in every six (6) to seven (7) year period.

Dischargeable Debts

Chapter 7 Bankruptcy relieves you from debt pertaining to:

- Credit cards
- Unsecured loans (no collateral pledged) from banks, credit unions, savings and loans, or finance companies.
- Unpaid hospital or physicians' bills
- Unpaid utility bills

Non-Dischargeable Debts

Debts that are not eliminated are:

- State and federal taxes
- Certain secured loans
- Child support required by law
- Spousal support (alimony) payments required by law
- Government-backed college loans (only dischargeable in special circumstances)
- Debts due to fraud
- Liability from damages resulting from willful or malicious acts
- Drunk driving obligations

CHAPTER 11-REORGANIZATION

Chapter 11 is typically used for businesses. It allows businesses to remain operational while:

- reorganizing debt by shedding burdensome leases and contracts
- recovering assets
- optimizing operations to become more profitable
- discharging certain debts
- and/or repaying an agreed upon portion of the total debt to creditors

Chapter 11 was originally designed for large corporate debtors, but is now available to partnerships, real estate developers and sole proprietors.

Chapter 12- Adjustment of Debts of a Family Farmer with Regular Annual Income

Chapter 12 was established specifically for farmers in 1986. This chapter allows farmers to repay current debt with future earnings. It is very similar to 13 in that farmers are allowed to devise a plan to repay certain debts and discharge others over time. The advantage of Chapter 12 is that it acknowledges the fact that most farmers need more credit than most consumers, the seasonal nature of agricultural income and the challenge of forecasting the profitability of crops. If the farmer's debt does not exceed $1,500,000, then they are eligible for Chapter 12 bankruptcy.

CHAPTER 13- ADJUSTMENT OF DEBTS OF AN INDIVIDUAL WITH REGULAR INCOME

Chapter 13 is another very common bankruptcy option, which is utilized by approximately 25% of consumers. The Chapter allows debtors to propose a repayment plan to cure debt over a period of time. It was designed for debtors who currently have a source of steady income and can repay creditors (usually $0.10 on the dollar) based on a proposed court approved repayment plan. The difference between Chapter 13 and Chapter 7 is that individuals are usually allowed to keep their possessions versus liquidating them. Therefore, debtors typically continue to reside in their homes unless they fail to comply with the arrangement. Another variation is the timing required to be completely discharged from all debt. Generally, debts are not discharged in Chapter 13 until all guidelines of the plan have been met, yet the chapter allows more debts to be eliminated than a Chapter 7 discharge.

Fees and Legal Help

When considering filing for bankruptcy, seek an experienced bankruptcy attorney for advice. If you need to obtain a referral in your state, contact the Bar Association's referral service. In the State of Texas, contact the State Bar of Texas Lawyer Referral Service by calling (800) 252-9690. Contact several attorneys to see if they charge for initial appointments, and to interview them prior to deciding to utilize their services.

When interviewing, remember to ask the following questions:

- What information should you bring to the initial consultation?
- How much experience do they have with bankruptcy cases?
- What percentage of their cases is similar to my specific situation?
- What is their success rate?
- Will other attorney advocates work on the case, or will the hired attorney perform all research and negotiations? If others will perform work, who are they and what are their fees?
- Are they attorneys or non-attorneys? What is their level of expertise and experience?
- What obstacles do they foresee with your case?
- Will counsel be provided based on realistic expectations of your current situation?
- What are their fees? Are they negotiable? Do they provide payment plans? (Get an estimated cost range in writing)
- Are there tasks that you can carry out to reduce the fee?
- Can they provide a list of client references?
- Are you available to take the case immediately?

- If questions arise, will you be able to contact them directly? How often? What times are best? (This question is particularly important if you would like to have lots of interaction with your attorney)

If you do not feel comfortable with a particular attorney, continue looking. However, once you find a lawyer that you feel comfortable with, be prepared to honestly and completely disclose all family assets, liabilities and commitments in order to obtain a comprehensive assessment.

In Texas, bankruptcy-filing fees could range from:

Chapter 7	$ 335.00
Chapter 9	$ 1,717.00
Chapter 11 (non-railroad)	$ 1,717.00
Chapter 11 (railroad)	$ 1,550.00
Chapter 12	$ 275.00
Chapter 13	$ 310.00

FORECLOSURE AUCTION

If you anticipate receiving a large sum of money, such as cash settlement from a lawsuit or a tax refund, then buying your house back at the foreclosure auction may be the answer you've been looking for. You must be in a position to pay the total bid price in cash or by cashier's check, usually within 30 minutes of winning the bid.

The date and location of the foreclosure auction varies from state to state, however in Texas, the auction is held every first Tuesday of the month at the county courthouse. Trustees and investors are often chaotically scattered throughout the room; therefore, it is very important that you attend the event with a game plan in mind. So now let's discuss what goes on at the auction and what the advantages are of attending the auction regardless of whether you have the cash to buy your house back or not.

Let's begin by discussing the roles of the primary players at the auction.

THE PLAYERS

Trustee: As mentioned previously, the Trustee is the one who holds legal title to your property for your lender. They make sure that you perform according to your obligation by verifying that payments are made to the lender on time. When you fail to make a payment, the trustee is the party who initiates foreclosure. At the auction the Trustee stands and reads the legal foreclosure notice -which may include the property address, owner's name, lenders name, and the opening bid. Only the trustee can conduct a valid foreclosure sale. If the original trustee cannot be present, a substitute may be appointed only by the party designated in the Deed of Trust.

It is important that you have a copy of the notice because the sale can be invalid for failure to comply with the Deed of Trust.

Real Estate Investors: Investors attend the event in order to acquire discounted homes that may be sold or rented to obtain a profit.

Homeowners: Several homeowners are present to purchase their houses at the auction or hear the amount of the winning bid.

THE DOCUMENTS

Acceleration Notice: This is the same notice of foreclosure that is forwarded to the homeowner, posted at the courthouse and recorded at the county clerk's office.

Trustee's Deed: When the property is sold at auction, the new owner receives this document as conveyance of ownership.

THE PROCESS

- The auction is held every first Tuesday of the month between 10 a.m. and 4 p.m. at the county courthouse where the property is located. Individual properties must be sold within three hours of the time stated in the acceleration notice.

- Trustees, generally located around the perimeter of the room, will stand in the midst of the crowd and read the posted foreclosure notice. At the Harris County auction, there is no podium, so you must pay close attention.

- The terms of sale will then be stated by the trustee.

- The trustee will begin the bidding process often by stating the lenders minimum bid. It is very important to know who's bid the trustee enters because it may not be the lender. They cannot place bids for themselves or for corporations that they control. They can however, place bids for the lender and third parties.

- Investors, homeowners and other interested parties call out their bids at random until the highest bid is reached.

- The investor or homeowner will then provide the required information to the Trustee or Trustee's representative, pay for the house using cash or cashier's checks and obtain a Trustee's Deed. No out of pocket costs are incurred if the lender is the highest bidder unless the bid price is greater than the balance of the debt.

- Proceeds from the sale are then distributed to cover the costs of 1) advertising, paying commission to the trustee, attorney's fees that are not covered by the lien, and any other expenses incurred to convey the property 2) the total principal balance, interest, and other charges and 3) any excess proceeds are distributed to the borrower.

The borrower is liable for any deficiency if the proceeds of the sale do not cover expenses in the first two groups. Should this occur, a deficiency judgment might be placed against the borrower by the lender in order to recoup these leftover costs. Deficiencies are based on Fair Market Value, which can be challenged by either party within 90 days of the sale or notice of the sale. (For detailed info check Chapter 51 of Texas Property Code)

STRATEGY

No one will look out *for* you quite *like* you, so attending the auction is always in your best interest. I say that because by attending you will know firsthand whether or not the house sold for more or less than the delinquent amount. If it sold for more (i.e. loan balance, delinquency, attorney's fees, etc.) then you should receive the excess. However, if the house is sold for less than you owe, then you may have to pay a deficiency judgment. By being present, you can also ensure that all bids are fairly recognized.

HOW TO PREPARE

- Purchase a foreclosure list from the courthouse in order to find out the time that your property will be up for auction. (This information should also be contained in the notices that you have received thus far).

- Know the current market value of your home, as well as the cost of repairs. If you do this, you'll have an advantage over all other bidders, because you'll have the inside scoop on just what the house is worth. It will also help you to determine the possible amount of deficiency if the house is sold for less than you owe.

- Set a bottom-line bid based on the market value minus the cost of repairs.

- Secure a video recorder so that you can record the auction. Therefore, if mistakes are made you will have proof.

- Arrive at least one hour before the listed auction time so that you can ask around to find out exactly where the trustee handling your mortgage will be located. Try to stand as close to the Trustee as possible so that you can hear all of the bids.

- If you plan to purchase your house at the auction, bring cashier's checks of various denominations (i.e. $500, $100, $50, etc.) because you will not receive change on the day of purchase. Be prepared to pay within thirty (30) minutes after winning the bid.

CHALLENGE THE LOAN DOCUMENTS

My job in writing this workbook is to provide all information that may be pertinent in helping you save your home. As a result, we'll discuss the last resort method of stopping foreclosure-- Contesting your loan documents in accordance with State and Federally Mandated Laws and Acts. When these Laws and Acts were created, the original intent was not to use them specifically as a means of stopping foreclosure, yet it has worked for others and it may just work for you.

Before I even begin discussing this topic, let me caution you to SEEK LEGAL COUNSEL to review your loan documents prior to moving forward with any claims. Just think about, if your lender –who creates these documents daily - made an error and didn't catch it, how likely is it that you will? Therefore, it is extremely important to obtain advice from an attorney who specializes in real estate law and is not only familiar with laws and Acts but has used them as a means of defense.

Think back to when you were a kid, and you got into a disagreement with the schoolyard bully or a sibling who was much larger than you. Your first reaction was probably to try to use reason and devise a solution that both of you could live with. If the other kid became totally unreasonable and began to push and shove, you would push and shove back, and it soon would turn into an all-out fight. Somewhere down the line you've learned to fight. Either your parents taught you or you took karate or boxing lessons, which taught you how to fight fairly. Yet, in the midst of fighting you might have realized (after being punched in the eye and seeing stars) that you were losing. We all know what usually happens next. The street fight - where you are determined to win at any cost.

That is the methodology behind the next tactic. It really isn't fair - like street fighting - because when you bought the house and the lender provided the funds, it was totally understood between both parties that the loan was to be repaid in a timely fashion. We all know that times and situations change and that you never imagined that you would be going through this when you bought the house. Now you've gone through the shoving, pushing and fighting fair stages with your lender and you're still penned between a rock and a hard place. That's when you proceed to commission an attorney to review your documents based on the following Acts. If errors are found the foreclosure process could be delayed temporarily, permanently, or the lender may owe you money instead of you owing them. The Acts that we will discuss are the Real Estate Settlement Procedures Act, Regulation Z of the Truth in Lending Act and Predatory Lending Laws.

REAL ESTATE SETTLEMENT PROCEDURES ACT (RESPA)

To begin, let's talk about the Real Estate Settlement Procedures Act. RESPA was first passed in 1974 and was instituted as a means of aiding consumers in shopping for settlement (closing) services and protecting them from unnecessary increases in certain costs associated with closing services.

The Act addresses the following topics:

• Closing Cost Disclosures	• Seller Required Title Insurance
• Lender Servicing Practices	• Limits on Escrow Accounts
• Escrow Account Practices	• Loan Servicing Complaints
• Prohibits kick-backs, referral fees and unearned fees	• Loan Servicing Transfers

We will not go into great detail regarding all topics, yet we'll highlight certain important aspects that may be helpful in stopping foreclosure. Specifically, we will discuss Section 6 - Loan Servicing Complaints and Section 10 - Limits on Escrow Accounts. If you would like to obtain more detailed information, visit http://www.hud.gov/offices/hsg/sfh/res/respamor.cfm.

There have been occurrences where homeowners were notified of foreclosure, yet they never missed a payment. In most of these instances, the loan was either transferred to another servicer without notifying the borrower or the borrower communicated issues or challenges to the lender that were never acknowledged.

In the event that your loan was transferred or sold to another servicer, your current loan servicer has an obligation to notify you of the change at least fifteen (15) days prior to the transfer or sell, in writing. The notice must contain the name, address, toll free number and the date in which the transfer will become effective and the new servicer should begin receiving payments. An important point to make here is that the borrower cannot be penalized as long as they send timely payments to the *old* servicer within sixty (60) days of the transfer.

Under Section 6 of RESPA, Lenders must respond in writing to *all* complaints by borrowers at least twenty (20) business days after receipt. They then have sixty (60) business days to rectify the problem or explain their position to the borrower in writing. The complaints may include payment posting disputes, customer service complaints, escrow account inquiries, and any other event or circumstance that poses a problem relating to your mortgage loan.

As a borrower, you have a right to file a lawsuit against any servicer who fails to comply with the provisions of Section 6.

As consumers, there are times when we are incorrectly charged or over charged without our knowledge because we don't know the rules. One place where you could be leaving money on the table is the escrow account that was probably set up when your loan was originated. RESPA doesn't require lenders to set up escrow accounts, yet several lenders do. Therefore, Section 10 of RESPA was created as a means of regulating the amount that lenders can require borrowers to place into escrow accounts. Each month the lender may require a borrower to pay into the escrow account no more than 1/12 of the total of all disbursements payable during the year, plus an amount necessary to pay for any shortage in the account. In addition, the lender may require a cushion, not to exceed an amount equal to 1/6 of the total disbursements for the year. If you've paid more than this amount, contact your lender because they may owe you a refund.

RESPA provides powerful tools for supporting consumers during situations of such disputes. However, the key to winning most disputes is to ensure that you are not in the wrong. To do so, CONTINUE making your regularly scheduled payments, and be able to provide supporting documents as evidence of your claim (i.e. letters, payment stubs, bank statements, receipts, conversation log - specifying when you called, who you spoke to, and what they said - and any other evidence that may be helpful).

REGULATION Z

In essence, Regulation Z of the Truth-in-Lending Act was created as a means of ensuring that potential borrowers understand their loan documents and can compare apples to apples when reviewing the terms and conditions of various loans. This is accomplished by requiring lenders to disclose such things as:

Lender's Name and Address for Monthly Payment Remittance	Total Amount Borrowed	Insurance Requirements	Payments Schedule	The Right Rescission
Amount Financed along with itemization	Late Payment Policy	Assumption Policy	Payment Amount	Disclosure of Terms and Conditions of ARM Loans
Annual Percentage Rate	Prepayment Policy	Contract Reference	Security Interest	
Maximum Interest Rate for Variable Rate Loans	Demand Features	Deposit Information	Security Interest Charges	

Regulation Z also requires lenders to disclose the information in a specific format, provide a preliminary disclosure within three (3) business days of receiving the application and a final disclosure at closing.

Frequent violations of Regulation Z are:

- Failure to provide such disclosures as a Good Faith Estimate, Special Information Booklet, Truth in Lending or a HUD-1 Settlement Statement
- Encouragement to provide false information on loan documents
- Requests to leave signature lines or other important fields blank
- Unexpected costs at closing that were not previously explained

Predatory Lending Laws

Another set of laws that were instituted to protect homeowners, are the Predatory Lending Laws. Predatory Lending Laws have been put into place to protect homeowners from intentional lender practices that could lead to foreclosure or other forms of financial hardship. Common predatory lending practices are:

- Loan underwriting that does not take into account the borrower's ability to repay. Borrowers typically qualify based on assets or equity versus income.

- Excessive loan fees or prepaid single premium insurance that is often added onto the principal balance and is considered part of the loan.

- Negative amortization. (Explanation: This occurrence is most common on adjustable rate loans. With these types of loans, borrowers have a monthly minimum payment like a credit card. If interest rates increase, the minimum payment may not cover the additional interest. Therefore, whatever amount is not paid will be added to your principal loan balance.)

- Prepayment penalties.

- High interest sub-prime loans to creditworthy borrowers who qualify for prime loans.

- Refinance restrictions on low cost loans.

- No mortgage counseling provided for loans with interest rates of 12% or greater.

There is a difference between a predatory lender and a lender that offers high interest rate loans. High interest loans are usually offered to individuals with less than perfect credit because of the lender's increased exposure to the risk of default. Predatory lenders prey on homeowners who customarily do not qualify for traditional loans. They not only charge excessive interest rates, but they also have unfair terms, conditions and other practices that can lead to hardship.

Several options have been provided. Now, circle all options that you would like to explore further. Then rank the circled options according to its feasibility and order in which you would like to discuss them with your lender, attorney, CPA, or real estate advisor.

Ranking	Option(s)
_____	Forbearance
_____	Temporary Indulgence
_____	Soldiers' and Sailors' Relief Act
_____	Repayment Plan
_____	Loan Modification
_____	Loan Restructuring
_____	Partial Claim
_____	Refinancing
_____	Payment Assistance
_____	Debt Consolidation
_____	Debt Consolidation Loans
_____	Natural Disaster
_____	Pre-foreclosure Sale
_____	Assumption
_____	Deed-in-lieu of Foreclosure
_____	Bankruptcy
_____	Purchase at Foreclosure Auction

NEGOTIATING WITH YOUR LENDER

Regardless of which option you chose of those provided, my first recommendation is that you contact your lender. Before you call, complete the following steps:

1) Complete the financial statement located in the Appendix to get an idea of where you are financially. Does your income exceed your expenses or is there too much month at the end of your money?

2) Create a hardship letter using the example located in the Appendix. The letter should provide details regarding your situation, and a plan on how you can bring the loan current. I don't know how often you work with lenders, but I can tell you that it's pretty tough to contact them and have a person-to-person conversation. That's why I'm instructing you to complete the above documents prior to calling them. Now as soon as they request these documents (which they will...trust me), you can fax them immediately if a fax machine is near.

3) Have your last two pay stubs, unemployment check stubs or other proof of current income handy (regardless of the dates).

Prior to the appointment, prepare at least five (5) or six (6) well thought out questions. Use these as a starting point:

- Will you please explain the foreclosure process?

- What options are available for saving my home?

- What options are available for selling my home?

- Are several borrowers experiencing problems with making on time mortgage payments due to the economic conditions?

- What is done with properties that the bank takes back at the foreclosure auction?

- Is it good business for lenders to foreclose or would they rather work with homeowners to generate a feasible solution?

Now that you have completed all of these actions, call the bank and ask to speak to the person in the loss mitigation department that is handling your account and deal directly with this person. If the person resides within the same city, schedule an appointment to speak to them in person as soon as possible. Take the following items to the meeting (I know that it is redundant, yet people do lose things so be prepared):

- Financial statement

- Hardship letter

- Proof of hardship (doctor's statement, letter from your job, etc.)

- Tax returns from the last two (2) years

- Last two (2) pay stubs, unemployment check stubs or other proof of current income

- Finally, a pen and pad for taking notes

When you meet with the lender, approach the individual with a thankful attitude. Tell them that you would like to brainstorm with them to identify possible solutions to reinstate your mortgage. Explain that you have run into a temporary problem, and that you are sure that they can show you some options that will allow you to recover your good standing with the lender. Make every effort to show them that you are a responsible person, and that you would like to obtain an outcome that is beneficial for both parties.

Throughout the conversation, write down each option as they are provided. When it appears as though the person has provided the last option say, "O.K. so it appears as though I have six options which are....1-2-3-4.... Are there any more options available?" As you repeat the options, be sure to also summarize your understanding of how the option works. If the individual fails to mention an option that is listed in this workbook, simply say, "Well, I've been told that other organizations offer...Do you provide this option also?" They may call the option by a different name or it may not be exactly the same, so it's best that you state the name given in this book as well as a description of what it entails. You can even take the workbook with you so that you don't have to try and memorize every little detail. This will also send a message to the lender that you are serious about saving your home. Once this is done, ask the lender: "What option would you recommend for my situation?"

After the two of you have discussed every possible option, and you are confident that you thoroughly understand the information provided, thank the person for their assistance and leave. Depending on where you are in the process, you do not have to make a rushed decision at that moment. Think about it overnight then the next day discuss the options with an attorney, C.P.A, or real estate advisor that is accustomed to dealing with owners whose houses are in foreclosure. Now make a decision. Win, lose, or draw, make a decision. This should only take three (3) days because remember you *only* have a total of forty-one (41) days. Some options take time to execute therefore you can't waste a lot of time toiling over a decision. Don't forget that if your house is sold at auction, you'll walk away with zero (0) to negative ten (-10).

Look at foreclosure on a scale from 10 to -10. With 10 being a plan that allows you to keep your home or sell it, start over, and not owe anyone anything and -10 being where you lose your house with nothing to show for it or even worse, still owing a deficiency judgment, where would you like to end up? Make a decision in three days. If the Loss Mitigator can't speak to you in person, talk to them on the phone until you feel comfortable, especially if your time is running out. Get it done, one way or the other.

If you experience an individual who is unwilling to accept your kind request for assistance, go back to the analogy above and begin street fighting. Here's how. Lay the notepad on their desk, take out a tape recorder and say, "It wouldn't bother you if I taped this, would it? I don't write very fast, and surely you want me to have record of all of the important points, don't you?" Then simply ask them the following questions:

- Is filing for bankruptcy one of my options?

- Can you provide a copy of my Regulation Z papers?

- Do you think that we can work together to identify a solution without filing for bankruptcy or bringing lawyers in to review the paperwork?

Now if you see that this approach is not working or if there is a positive change in the person's attitude, go back to being nice, warm and sincere.

Remember, be creative.

CONVERSATION LOG

It is extremely important that you keep a log of all conversations with your lender. Use the form below as a guide to ensure that you obtain information regarding when you called, whom you spoke to and what the representative said. For additional forms, see the appendix.

Date _____   Time _____

Representative's Name _____

Department _____

Direct Phone # (___) _____ - _____   Best Times to Call _____

REFERRALS

Name _____   Number (___) _____ - _____

Name _____   Number (___) _____ - _____

Name _____   Number (___) _____ - _____

Name _____   Number (___) _____ - _____

CONVERSATION:

_____

_____

_____

_____

_____

_____

_____

At this point, you have everything that you need to begin saving your home from foreclosure. Bear in mind that time is not on your side, so you must take action immediately. If you wait another day, you may greatly reduce your options and possibly lose your home. If you have questions regarding what you've read, or need assistance implementing your options. Please do not hesitate to email us at Support@BehindOnMortgagePayments.com visit our website at www.BehindOnMortgagePayments.com.

Recall, that there are six (6) ways to stop the clock at any time during the process. They are:

- Pay all back payments, late fees, penalties, and interest.

- Negotiate with the lender to extend, delay, or forgive the debt.

- Refinance

- Sell the House

- File for bankruptcy

- Challenging the trust deed if violations or discrepancies exist

If you execute at least one of these options, then you will achieve the goal of saving your house either permanently or temporarily. Just remember…

STOP Don't lose hope. Unless your house has been sold at auction, you still have options.

GO Make every effort to save your home and credit history if at all possible.

GO Contact your mortgage lender immediately to identify what options are available to save your property.

STOP Do not vacate the property. If you do, you may be disqualified for certain forms of assistance.

🟢 **GO** Seek professional advice from an attorney, CPA, credit counselor, or real estate professional that specializes in foreclosures or real estate prior to making a final decision. If you cannot afford to pay someone immediately, there are several groups that provide volunteer services or payment plans. Contact BehindOnMortgagePayments.com or a HUD-approved housing counselor and review the Appendix to obtain a list of local contacts.

🛑 **STOP** I know that you've received lots of mail, and even people knocking on your door stating that they would like to "help" you. Some of these individuals do approach you with a sincere heart to help. However, beware, because there are others who will prey on your lack of knowledge and steal your home… with your consent. That's why this workbook is so important. We teach you what others don't want you to know.

🛑 **STOP** Here's some good advice…. if you want to permanently relieve yourself of the mortgage, sell the house outright. DO NOT DEED THE PROPERTY TO SOMEONE ELSE BEFORE SEEKING LEGAL COUNSEL AND DRAFTING A CONTRACT THAT PROTECTS YOU FROM LOSSES. If you suspect a scam, visit http://LoanScamAlert.org.

🟢 **GO** Lastly, take action immediately! The foreclosure clock is ticking if a notice of default has been filed. If you choose to do nothing, you will lose your home, severely damage your credit rating, there may be tax consequences, and you will possibly still owe the lender if the house is sold at auction for less than you owe. Do not wait until the last minute. Your options decrease as time progresses, so seek help today.

APPENDIX

FORECLOSURE ASSISTANCE

BehindOnMortgagePayments.com offers a wide range of products and services including a step-by-step workbook, educational webinars, and an investor program. They are designed to make this often difficult and emotional process as easy as possible.

Our motto is, "*Be Creative*." Therefore, much of the information that we provide is geared toward giving homeowners an extra nudge when they feel as though they have exhausted all known options.

WORKBOOK

BehindOnMortgagePayments.com has created a simple, yet comprehensive workbook to guide homeowners step-by-step through the process of saving their property from foreclosure. The workbook focuses on revealing where they are now, and what they can do to stop the foreclosure process. It includes:

- SECRET STRATEGIES THAT LENDERS DON'T TELL YOU ABOUT!
- HOW TO STOP THE FORECLOSURE PROCESS IMMEDIATELY WITHOUT LOSING YOUR HOME!
- SOURCES OF FREE FAST CASH!
- HOW TO SELL YOUR HOUSE IN 7 DAYS!
- HOW TO NEVER GO INTO FORECLOSURE AGAIN!

ONLINE FORECLOSURE WEBINARS FOR HOMEOWNERS

The seminars are conducted as a means of educating homeowners about the options that are available if they are unable to fulfill their mortgage obligation. Much of the information provided within the workbook is included in the seminars, but I discuss specifics that are not covered here. I also walk you through each phase and demonstrate how to perform each step. Visit BehindonMortgagePayments.com.

SHORT SALE CONSULTATION

We also offer personal consultations to homeowners who have exhausted all options and are interested in selling their home. With this service, our consultants work directly with clients to create a step-by-step customized plan that includes an informal desktop valuation to identify the existing value of the house and recommendations on how to move forward. This service also contains recommendations to help you identify viable options from scams. Contact us today by calling (713) 903-7107. EVEN IF YOU DO NOT USE US, ALWAYS GET A SECOND OPINION.

INVESTOR PROGRAM

Lastly, helping owners save their homes is our first priority. If that goal is unattainable, we allow you to advertise your house for sale on our website free of charge. This allows you to locate investors that can move quickly and are interested in purchasing property to prevent foreclosure.

PRODUCT & SERVICES PRICING

Product/Service	Price
How NOT to Lose Your Home	$47.00
Webinar: How to Stop Foreclosure	FREE
Short Sale Consultation	FREE
Cash Flow Analysis Calculator	$4.97
Personal Financial Statement Calculator	$4.97
Sample Hardship Letters	$4.97
Questions for Your Lender, Agent, Bankruptcy Attorney, CPA, Investors and More	$4.97
How to Keep Your Home Bundle: (Get Workbook, Video Guidance, Calculators and All Documents)	$97
The Docs Bundle: (Get Calculators and All Documents)	$9.97

Place all orders at http://www.behindonmortgagepayments.com/shop • or
Email us at Support@BehindOnMortgagePayments.com

IMPORTANT INFORMATION ABOUT HOUSING COUNSELING

BehindonMortgagePayments.com is not a loan or mortgage company, real estate brokerage firm, licensed attorney, tax advisor/accountant or a HUD Approved Housing Counseling Agency. We are homeowners who survived the foreclosure of our homes, and came together to teach you how to do the same.

We do not guarantee any specific results or outcomes. We cannot guarantee that you will be able to qualify for a loan product or refinance or modify your exiting loan or arrange to keep your home.

If you prefer assistance in a language other than English, please visit https://apps.hud.gov/offices/hsg/sfh/hcc/hcs.cfm, click on your state and select an agency that offers your language.

The information presented in this workbook, during your housing counseling session and in any follow-up communications is based on information you provided and other factors. We do not guarantee the applicability, accuracy, availability or your eligibility for any product, service or program mentioned.

Housing counseling is NOT a substitute for legal advice from a licensed attorney, or tax and financial advice from an accountant. If you need help understanding how the law applies to your particular circumstances and what is best financially for you and your family, you should seek the information from a qualified attorney or accountant.

INTERNET RESOURCES

How NOT to Lose Your Home	www.BehindOnMortgagePayments.com
City of Houston	www.cityofhouston.gov/
Goose Creek CISD Tax Office	www.goosecreek.cisd.esc4.net/right.htm
Harris County	www.co.harris.tx.us
Harris County Tax Assessor-Collector	www.tax.co.harris.tx.us/forms/ac-501.pdf
Harris County Appraisal District	www.hcad.org/
Houston Real Time Traffic map	www.mbaker.net/houston/info/traffic.htm
State of Texas	www.state.tx.us/
Texas A & M Real Estate Center	http://recenter.tamu.edu/
Weather from EMWIN Houston	www.emwin.org/
County Clerk's Home Page	www.cclerk.hctx.net/
Public Records Online	www.courthousedirect.com/
Website & Language Translations	http://babelfish.altavista.com/
Texas Marriage Records	www.tdh.state.tx.us/bvs/default.htm
Texas Divorce Records	www.cdc.gov
Homes and Communities	www.hud.gov/
Fannie Mae Home Page	www.fanniemae.com/
Recent Housing Statistics	www.texashousing.org/
Predatory Lending	www.hud.gov/offices/hsg/pred/predlend.cfm
Protecting a Home's Equity	www.bankrate.com
Home Buyer Glossary	www.buyersresource.com/Bglossary.html
State Information	www.state.tx.us
Volunteer Attorneys	www.ehvlp.org/index.html
County Data	www.txcountydata.com
Tax Information	www.taxnetusa.com/
Texas Association of Realtors	https://www.texasrealestate.com/
Consumer Protection	https://www.ftc.gov/about-ftc/bureaus-offices/bureau-consumer-protection
Better Business Bureau	www.bbb.org
Average Closing Costs	www.hsh.com/cfee-sample.html

SOCIAL ORGANIZATIONS: MONETARY ASSISTANCE

Several local social organizations provide monetary assistance to people who are facing hard times. Most of these organizations require that you are presently going through foreclosure. You can solicit funds from more than one organization; however, you must be able prove that balance can be paid in full if funds are received. To review additional organizations, visit https://www.needhelppayingbills.com

Agencies/Programs LOCATED IN Houston offering Mortgage Assistance

AIDS Foundation Houston, Inc.
AIDS Foundation Houston, Inc.
3202 Wesleyan Annex Houston, TX 77027
Emergency Food Shelter Program (EFSP)   (713) 623-6796
Financial Assistance

Bear Creek Assistance Ministries
16209 Keith Harrow Houston, TX 77084
Emergency Food Shelter Program (EFSP)   (281) 855-0014
Financial Assistance
LANGUAGES: Spanish

Brentwood Baptist Church
13033 Landmark Street Houston, TX 77045
Rent and Mortgage Assistance   (713) 852-1429

Catholic Charities of the Diocese of Galveston-Houston
Guadalupe Area Social Services
326 South Jensen Houston, TX 77003
Family Assistance   (713) 227-9981
Financial Assistance
LANGUAGES: Spanish

Christian Community Service Center, Inc.
Christian Community Service Center - Branard Street Office
3434 Branard Houston, TX 77027
Emergency Services   (713) 871-9741

Community Family Centers, Inc.
7524 Avenue E Houston, TX 77012
Emergency Food Shelter Program (EFSP)   (713) 923-2316
Financial Assistance

Gulf Coast Community Services Association
5000 Gulf Freeway, Building 1 Houston, TX 77023
Rent and Mortgage Assistance   (713) 393-4700

Harris County Social Services
Harris County Social Services

9418 Jensen Houston, TX 77093
Social and Financial Services **(713) 696-7900**

Harris County Social Services
Harris County Social Services - Downtown Satellite Office
1310 Prairie, Suite 1000 Houston, TX 77002
Social and Financial Services **(713) 696-7900**

Harris County Social Services
Harris County Social Services - Northwest Satellite Office
15555 Kuykendahl Houston, TX 77090
Social and Financial Services **(713) 696-7900**

Harris County Social Services
Harris County Social Services - Sunnyside Satellite Office
4605 Wilmington Houston, TX 77051
Social and Financial Services **(713) 696-7900**

Lutheran Social Services of the South, Inc.
Ruth's House Assistance Ministry
10260 North Freeway Houston, TX 77037
Emergency Services **(281) 999-1122**

Northwest Assistance Ministries
15555 Kuykendahl Houston, TX 77090
Emergency Food Shelter Program (EFSP) **(281) 885-4500**
Emergency Financial Aid
LANGUAGES: Spanish

Spring Woods United Methodist Church
1711 F.M. 1960 West Houston, TX 77090
Rent and Mortgage Assistance **(281) 444-6468**

The Salvation Army - Houston Metropolitan Area Command
1500 Austin Street Houston, TX 77002
Social Services **(713) 752-0686**

Wesley Community Center, Inc.
1410 Lee Street Houston, TX 77009
Emergency Food Shelter Program (EFSP) **(713) 223-8131**
Emergency Assistance

West Houston Assistance Ministries
10501 Meadowglen Houston, TX 77042
CARE Ministry **(713) 977-9942**
Emergency Assistance
LANGUAGES: Spanish

Wheeler Avenue Baptist Church
Social Services Center
3812 Wheeler Avenue Houston, TX 77004
Financial Assistance for Utilities **(713) 747-7101**
Utility Bill Assistance

Agencies/Programs LOCATED OUTSIDE Missouri City offering Mortgage Assistance

Fort Bend County Social Services
4520 Reading Road, Suite A Rosenberg, TX 77471
Rent and Mortgage Assistance (281) 342-7300
LANGUAGES: Spanish
Emergency Food Shelter Program (EFSP) (281) 342-7300
Financial Assistance

East Fort Bend Human Needs Ministry, Inc.
425 Stafford Run Road Stafford, TX 77477
Financial Assistance (281) 261-5470
LANGUAGES: Spanish

Agencies/Programs LOCATED IN Galveston offering Mortgage Assistance

Catholic Charities of the Diocese of Galveston-Houston
Galveston Office
4418 Avenue M, Suite 1 Galveston, TX 77550
Family Assistance (409) 762-2143

Galveston County Social Services
123 Rosenberg, Suite 4020 Galveston, TX 77550
Emergency Assistance (409) 770-5583

Agencies/Programs LOCATED OUTSIDE Galveston offering Mortgage Assistance

Galveston County Social Services
League City Office
174 Calder Road, Suite 142 League City, TX 77573
Emergency Assistance (281) 316-8733

Catholic Charities of the Diocese of Galveston-Houston
Texas City Satellite Office
Confidential Address Texas City, TX 77591
Family Assistance (409) 762-2143
Financial Assistance

Galveston County Social Services
Texas City Office
2516 Texas Avenue Texas City, TX 77590
Emergency Assistance (409) 770-5803

Agencies/Programs LOCATED IN Houston offering Legal Information Lines

Houston Bar Association
1001 Fannin, Suite 1300 Houston, TX 77002
Legal Line (713) 759-1133
Legal Services
LANGUAGES: Spanish, Vietnamese

Houston Volunteer Lawyers Program
712 Main Street, 27th Floor Houston, TX 77002
Family & Elder Law Programs; Legal Services	**(713) 228-0732**

Texas Human Rights Foundation
803 Hawthorne Houston, TX 77006
Legal Services	**(713) 522-0636**

Agencies/Programs LOCATED IN Houston offering Lawyer Referral Service

Houston Lawyer Referral Service, Inc.
1001 Fannin, Suite 1370 Houston, TX 77002
Lawyer Referral and Information Service	**(713) 237-9429**

Agencies/Programs LOCATED OUTSIDE Houston offering Lawyer Referral Service

Christian Legal Resource Center
1314 Winchester Conroe, TX 77385
Legal Services	**(936) 321-2643**

Agencies/Programs LOCATED IN Houston offering Home Rehabilitation/Repair

Houston Area Urban League
1301 Texas Avenue Houston, TX 77002
Home Repair	**(713) 393-8730**
Home Rehabilitation
LANGUAGES: Spanish

Agencies/Programs LOCATED IN Houston offering Home Maintenance Services

PSI HomeSavers
1111 Fannin, Suite 1335 Houston, TX 77002
Interior Repair Program	**(713) 659-2511**
Home Rehabilitation
Roofs Over Houston	**(713) 659-2511**
Home

Agencies/Programs LOCATED IN Houston offering Home Rehabilitation/Repair Grants

City of Houston, Department of Housing and Community Development
601 Sawyer, 4th Floor Houston, TX 77007
Houston HomeTown	**(713) 868-8400**
Financial Assistance
LANGUAGES: French, Spanish

Harris County Housing and Economic Development
Harris County Housing and Economic Development
8410 Lantern Point Houston, TX 77054
Housing Rehabilitation Program	**(713) 578-2000**
Home Rehabilitation

REFERENCES

Buck, Craig E., Anderson, Teri L. "How to Assume the Non-Assumable Loan: Contracts for Deed." 2000.

    02 June 2003 <http://members.aol.com/ReaLawBuck/KD.html>

Fambrough, Judon. "A Homeowner's Rights Under Foreclosure." Real Estate Center, October, 1996: 2-8

"Avoid Foreclosure Overview." Quinn, Ryan. Fannie Mae. Fanniemae.com.

    13 May 2018. < https://www.knowyouroptions.com/avoid-foreclosure-overview >

"Avoiding Foreclosure." HUD. HUD.gov: n.d, n.p.

    3 July 2019 < https://www.hud.gov/topics/avoiding_foreclosure >

"Closing Costs". Max Exchange Real Estate Network. Maxexchange.com.

    11 Nov. 2003 <http://www.maxexchange.com/real_estate_network/closing_costs.htm>

"RESPA: More about RESPA: The Real Estate Settlement Procedures Act." HSH Associates. n.d.

    04 February 2010 http://library.hsh.com/articles/government-programs/respa-the-real-estate-settlement-procedures-act/

"Understanding Your Foreclosure Rights: A Consumer Law Review" Credit.com

    11 Nov. 2016 <https://www.credit.com/debt/understanding-your-foreclosure-rights/>

"The Average Cost of Foreclosure". Pocket Sense. PockeSense.com

27 July 2019 < https://pocketsense.com/average-cost-foreclosure-8621045.html>

www.ingramcontent.com/pod-product-compliance
Lightning Source LLC
Chambersburg PA
CBHW081327190426
43193CB00043B/2836